O9-AIE-703

# Conversations That Get Results and Inspire Collaboration

## Engage Your Team, Your Peers, and Your Manager to Take Action

## Shawn Kent Hayashi

New York   Chicago   San Francisco   Lisbon   London   Madrid   Mexico City
Milan   New Delhi   San Juan   Seoul   Singapore   Sydney   Toronto

Copyright © 2013 by Shawn Kent Hayashi. All rights reserved. Printed in the United States of America. Except as permitted under the United States Copyright Act of 1976, no part of this publication may be reproduced or distributed in any form or by any means, or stored in a data base or retrieval system, without prior written permission of the publisher.

1 2 3 4 5 6 7 8 9 0 FGR/FGR 1 8 7 6 5 4 3

ISBN: 978-0-07-180593-3
MHID: 0-07-180593-1

e-ISBN: 978-0-07-180594-0
e-MHID: 0-07-180594-X

This publication is designed to provide accurate and authoritative information in regard to the subject matter covered. It is sold with the understanding that neither the author nor the publisher is engaged in rendering legal, accounting, or other professional service. If legal advice or other expert assistance is required, the services of a competent professional person should be sought.
> —*From a Declaration of Principles Jointly Adopted by a Committee of the American Bar Association and a Committee of Publishers and Associations*

McGraw-Hill books are available at special quantity discounts to use as premiums and sales promotions, or for use in corporate training programs. To contact a representative, please e-mail us at bulksales@mcgraw-hill.com.

This book is printed on acid-free paper.

*Dedicated to Jane Firth,*
*who inspired me with her amazing listening ability.*
*She role-models the best deep listening and inspires*
*meaningful collaborations as a result.*

# Acknowledgments

Thank you to Angela Rice, William Hagan, Michelle Staas, Kate Early, Ann Strini, Dave Rees, Robert Andrucci, Caroline Nawrocki, and Bill Tyson for reading and rereading with me as this book evolved. Your fingerprints are all over this work.

On a project like this there are so many people behind the scenes whose names do not show up here. To all my clients and colleagues, thank you. Our conversations inspire me.

To the winners of the Star Developer Award and your commitment to developing future leaders in your organizations, you inspire collaboration in meaningful ways. Thank you.

To my colleagues, students, and friends at the Lehigh University MBA program, including Andrew Ward, Brandon Gallagher, and Mary Gulick, thank you for your support and the provocative conversations during our dinners and classes.

My respect and gratitude to all my friends who participate in the Business Banter Discussion group at Saucon Valley Country Club. A special mention to Sy and Sue Traub, Alan and Kathy Sterner, Joseph and Sara Perrotta, Michael and Heidi Schiffman, and Luis and Christine Alvarez. You are cherished friends.

Bob Diforio, Mary Glenn, and Casey Ebro, I am blessed to be able to collaborate with you again.

Elizabeth Jeffries, Anne-Mette Halvorson, Jane Firth, and Alan Weiss, you inspire me and continue to be cherished friends. Thank you for sharing your wisdom.

Jim Hayashi, thank you for everything you do to support me! I am deeply grateful for you.

# Contents

PART 1

## THE FOUNDATION FOR
## SUCCESSFUL COLLABORATION

# Preface

Heidi Schiffman had a vision to run a for-profit, successful business that also raised money for schools. She launched this business in 1993. Fast-forward to today: Heidi is founder and President of KidStuff. As a wildly successful business, KidStuff has raised more than $40 million for education. Its business model is easy to understand: KidStuff provides a way for schools to raise money for classroom supplies, field trips, computers, sports equipment, and anything else they would like for students. The school earns 50 percent profit or more on every $25 KidStuff Coupon Book that is sold. When I asked Heidi what she believes is the key to KidStuff's success, she said, "Collaboration. Everything we do is done in teams. We have the conversations we need to have to keep growing. We have high-performing teams within our organization, and we show schools how to create collaboration focused on a positive vision in their own communities." Heidi knows teams perform better than groups of individual contributors, and high-performing teams create a great organization.

Heidi realized she would not be able to bring her vision to life by herself. KidStuff became a success growing into 17 marketplaces because people were inspired to work together around a common goal to make a positive difference.

Have you ever wondered how someone like Heidi creates a successful company that makes a positive difference in the world? Would you like to know how people like this create communities of action that get amazing results? I'm going to show you how to engage yourself, your team, your peers, and your manager to get results.

Are you a team member, a peer, or a leader? Perhaps you play all three roles. Would you like to know how to engage in conversations effectively, with awareness of the role you are playing and its impact on what works best? This is a unifying thread you will find throughout the book, as we explore each role and the ways to engage others based on the role you are now playing. Your role may determine what is expected of you—sometimes you are expected to create and communicate the goals, and other times you are expected to align your work around existing goals that a leader or team in your organization created. After reading this book you will have the awareness and confidence to create the right conversation at the right time, based on your role.

With this book you now have an executive coach guiding you through a series of conversations to develop your abilities. I'm sharing with you the exact conversations I have with my executive coaching clients and saving you thousands of dollars.

At the end of each chapter you will find a section called "Application Exercise." There I'll be asking you to apply the ideas you read about and to think about how they affect your peers, your team members, and your boss. By completing these application exercises, you will become a better collaborator and achieve higher-level results. I've watched over and over as my coaching clients grew to higher levels of business maturity by applying the ideas from these assignments.

—Shawn Kent Hayashi

# THE FOUNDATION FOR SUCCESSFUL COLLABORATION

*Leadership is often too focused on analysis and data, but today there is a greater need for: building trust, defining our purpose, appreciating contributions, and giving encouragement. These are the foundation for collaboration.*
—Stephen G. Hart, AVP Human Resources, Federal Reserve Bank of Philadelphia

# Knowing What You Want to Create

Business is a conversation focused on creating results.

Being successful in business begins in a conversation with ourselves first, and then with others, focused on what we are passionate about creating, about the solutions we want to bring alive, and the way we want to add value and serve others. Successful professionals invite their teams, peers, and managers to align their own individual goals and motivators to the rewards of the project they are engaged in. Wildly successful business leaders create conversations with others by inspiring passion for the value and services they can deliver working together.

Like most senior executives, Larry Page, the cofounder and CEO of Google, began 2012 by sharing his goals for the company. He said, "Google is a large company now, but we will achieve more, and do it faster, if we approach life with the passion and soul of a start-up." He went on to outline six core areas of focus for the upcoming year. If you worked for or with Google during that time, it would be important that you understood these goals and how they affected what you were doing as an employee, team member, manager, leader, or even supplier. At Google, your ability to engage in conversations and demonstrate results around these desired goals determines your success.

If you work for or with General Mills, you know that one of their most talked-about goals is to be among the most socially responsible food companies in the world. General Mills says, "We continually set targets for bettering the nutritional profile of our foods, and we keep addressing social and environmental challenges." They made it clear that this is a conversation they want to further, and people who are passionate about bettering the nutritional profile of food and who want to collaborate around this topic would be engaged working with General Mills. To be successful in this organization, you have to demonstrate how your actions and results align with the company goals, no matter if you are a team member, peer, leader, or supplier.

Collaboration revolves around having meaningful conversations focused on achieving results with other people. Your role will determine what part you play in creating the vision. If you are the leader, you must clearly define and then communicate the outcomes you are committed to creating. If you report to a leader, understanding what the leadership team of the business you work for sees as important will enable you to link the business focus to your own goals in meaningful ways. If you are a peer of someone who works in another department or division of the same company, it will be important for you to understand the results other teams are expected to produce. Fully engaging leaders, peers, and team members evolve as a result of having a shared purpose.

To have engaging, meaningful conversations with others, you'll need to know what motivates you and how you prefer to communicate. You will need to clarify your own goals before you communicate them effectively to others. People who know themselves well focus on the question, "What do I want to create?"

As an executive coach, when I begin working with a new client I ask, "What do you really want to create now? And why?" I also explain that, if you do not know the answer to those questions, you are likely to be working and living someone else's agenda for your career and life. Investing in yourself or paying yourself first is not a new idea in business—it is how wildly wealthy people and businesses became what they are. When you have a clear and compelling vision for what you want to create, you are investing in yourself and your future. Then you will be able to make a greater contribution to a business or team, and be a better leader.

I encourage my coaching clients to create their own "That's for Me!" lists. Here is how you can do this too: Go to a place you enjoy, where you can relax and feel great. Design on paper what you want your business and life to include and who you want to be. Make a list of 100 experiences, things, opportunities, and conversations you want to have, and places you want to go. Include the ways in which you want to serve other people in your work. How do you want to add value? Also include the people you want to meet. Whom do you want to support, guide, and mentor? Identify the story you want to be known for, and put that on your list too. As you construct this list, you begin to own your agenda and gain clarity about what you want to create in your life and your work. By developing this list over time, you begin to see what will motivate and inspire you, so that you can be passionate about your work. Have you noticed that the people who are star performers are usually passionate about their whole lives? That is why I'm suggesting as your first assignment that you focus your "That's for Me!" list on your business and personal life, because successful people have integrated the two together.

Almost every time I give this exercise to people who have never done it before, they say something like, "I can't come up with 100. I have 20 and I'd be happy with those." To which I reply: "I asked you to identify at least 100, and you are making your life smaller. You are choosing a glass ceiling for yourself. Why would you want to do that?" Push yourself through this activity, and you will see amazing things begin to happen that you cannot imagine now. You will have more clarity about what you want and what inspires you to take action.

As we work together over several months I frequently share this reminder: Once you have created your list, begin to read it regularly. Keep adding to it as you come across things you are passionate about. Make sure all the results you want to create in your business are on your list. Many of my coaching clients read their lists every day as they are learning to think in new ways and to focus on results that align with their agendas. I read my own list at least once per week to stay focused on the priorities that are most important to me. Amazing things begin to happen when you focus on your goals and what you want to create.

Maintain your list in an electronic document. Once you have completed an item, move it to the end of the file under the heading "I did it!" By doing this, eventually you will have pages and pages of items on your "I did it!" list. It is very fulfilling to review that list, as it shows momentum and the ability to get results.

When people look closely at their "That's for Me!" list, there is something that will jump out quickly: In order to accomplish many items on your list, you'll discover you have to engage other people. You will have to inspire others to join you in your endeavors. *That is why we collaborate!*

## Engage Your Team, Your Peers, and Your Manager to Take Action

Why do you think your team, your peers, and your manager may want to help you achieve what is on your list? Most people have a desire to interact with others and to cocreate. In the first part of this book, I will show you how to identify and explain why helping you will benefit your peers, your manager, and your team, in language they will understand. I'll also show you how to build relationships and be engaging when you meet with new people, based on their communication styles and motivators.

Figuring out where to go next and what actions will create momentum comes from building a strong mental muscle, which keeps you focused on clarifying and distinguishing what you want to create next. Building your "That's for Me!" list over time gives you this focus and builds this mental muscle. Clarity about whom you will want to collaborate with will guide you to build new relationships with stakeholders, allies, and sponsors. You'll need to understand how to read their communication styles and motivators and create meaningful conversations that engage them. That is where we are going next. But first, take the time to complete the application exercise, and you will gain the benefits you would experience from working with an executive coach.

## Knowing What You Want to Create Application Exercise

Create your own "That's for Me!" list. Ask yourself, "What results, experiences, or accomplishments would trigger in me feelings of excitement, passion, and jubilation?"

Identify the goals of the business you work with, and consider how your passions fit with the corporate focus.

Think about the various roles you currently play: employee, peer, manager, etc. For each role ask yourself these questions:

What are the results you are committed to already in this role?

With whom do you already collaborate in this role?

With whom would you like to collaborate?

Can you think of someone who would benefit from helping you bring alive the items on your "That's for Me!" list?

# CHAPTER 2

# People Reading: Preferred Communication Styles

We read to comprehend the information we are focused on. When interacting with people, we need the skills to comprehend other people's frames of reference, how they like to make decisions, how they prefer to respond to challenges, the pace of their environments, and the way they will respond to rules set by others. We also need to be able to see their motivators and the effects of their emotions as they relate to what they want to listen to and what will engage them. I call this "people reading."

To bring your "That's for Me!" list alive, you will need to identify who would enjoy creating with you and who will be willing to engage with you in a meaningful way. Getting others to focus on your desired results and take the right actions requires learning how to "people read," so you can select the best bosses, colleagues, mentors, and team members for you. These are the people who will encourage you to grow, based on your goals and vision for your life, and you will do the same for them.

There are three parts to people reading:

**Communication style:** *how* you approach others

**Motivators:** *why* you do what you do

**Emotional intelligence:** your ability to use your feelings *wisely* to guide your actions and make better decisions

In this section, I am going to reveal what you need to know in order to be able to people read anyone you meet. As you become a master of this skill, you will be able to identify and develop other people's strengths and make your "That's for Me!" list come true, by collaborating effectively with the right people at the right time.

Recently I was asked, "What is the number one most important skill that people need to develop to be successful in business today?" I replied without hesitating, "The ability to people read, so effective communication occurs no matter what role we are playing."

When you have the ability to identify another person's preferred communication style, workplace motivators, and current emotion, you will have better conversations and be more effective. You will collaborate, lead, coach, manage, and serve in meaningful ways, by adapting to the communication needs of the moment. You will experience more effective communication and relationships than you have ever known before. Magic will happen around you, because you are making connections that matter.

Lee Iacocca says, "Communication is *everything*!" I would add that the right communication that connects with your listener is everything.

People dynamics—interpersonal communication—has patterns similar to dance moves. If you understand these patterns, you will be more effective in dancing the steps effectively. If you do not understand these patterns, your communication, like your dance movements, can seem disjointed and awkward, putting you at risk of doing the "cotton-eye Joe" when everyone else is dancing the "dougie."

People reading includes seeing clusters of behaviors and motivators and using this awareness in the conversations you have with others. Understanding the range of behaviors and motivators will guide you to recognize what is likely to emerge in a relationship. People reading gives you the self-awareness to be sensitive to the communication needs of others, so your message will reach them—so they will understand you. For example, someone who likes to make decisions quickly and forcefully will also probably like a strong, healthy debate—in other words, he or she will enjoy what people who do not like to make quick decisions call arguing. On the other hand, someone who prefers to research a broad array of options, perhaps reading several books or articles on the topic before making a decision, will probably not like a strong emotional appeal in your presentation. When you have memorized the cluster patterns and how they fit together, you will begin to see and then read these people dynamics. As a team member, you will solve people problems in teams by filling in the missing pieces. As a leader, you will put the right people in roles that will bring out their best selves and help you achieve the goals that are most meaningful to you.

As with any new skill, learning this one requires you to understand the model and then practice, practice, practice until you master it. So let's begin with exploring the people-reading model. There are three parts. First, we will focus on identifying preferred communication styles, then in the next chapter I'll show you how to identify motivators, and finally, you'll learn how to practice using your emotions as a guidance system.

## Preferred Communication Styles

First, imagine that there are four common patterns in wiring a human brain that result in preferred conversation behavior and stories. Or you could think of it as four different windows people look out of as they communicate.

Each of the following represents a different communication window:

Direct, results-oriented, action-focused, and forceful conversations

Optimistic, fun, creative, entertaining, expressive, and lively conversations

Relaxed, patient, steady, and process-oriented conversations

Fact-based, accurate, logical, analytical, and detail-oriented conversations

Imagine these as communication windows that you look through as you interact with others. Depending on which window you are looking out of, you are going to see, experience, and want different things. When you have mastered this, you will be able to select the communication window that you need at the moment in order to achieve the best outcome, rather than doing what comes to you most naturally.

There is not one right way for us to behave or communicate, so there is not one style of communication that will be best in all situations. The goal is to understand these four patterns of brain-wiring. When you do, you will be able to identify in a meeting or a conversation what the underlying conversation needs are for each person to be able to walk away from the exchange feeling that things are moving forward. When you identify the needs clearly, you can decide whether you are the right person to provide that information, or if you would be better served by finding someone with a different communication style who can achieve the desired results.

Let's take this deeper now.

When looking to identify which communication style is being displayed, ask yourself these two questions:

• Is the person (or group) I am communicating with more outgoing and extroverted, or more internal and introverted?

- Is the person (or group) I am communicating with more task-focused or more people-focused?

Outgoing or extroverted communicators tend to speak directly, loudly, with crisp, sharp, or large circular gestures. They enjoy meeting and talking with people and will be proactive in meeting new people. Gregarious, animated, or bold are words that may be used to describe their behavior. They will jump in and start a conversation quickly, adding their own ideas, opinions, and suggestions. Groups of meeting planners, sales teams, and advertising executives commonly are outgoing communicators.

Internal or introverted communicators tend to speak softly, indirectly with small or no hand gestures. To people with another style they may appear timid or shy at first and tend to wait until they are introduced to engage in conversation. Diplomatic, reserved, and thoughtful are words that may be used to describe their behavior. They will likely wait until someone else initiates a conversation, and then they will respond. Groups of research scientists, chemical engineers, and accountants commonly are introverted communicators.

Task-focused communicators may have checklists for everything. They are focused on the current process and task at hand. People using a task focus will dive into the work or business agenda immediately. They appear to want to check items off the list and move onto the next item. They do not appear to want to engage in small talk until after the work is finished.

Here are examples of what this sounds like:

"Tally the five rows on this spreadsheet, then analyze which data we will use in our report."

"Read this report and summarize the three key points."

"Send me the process flow on this project plan."

People-focused communicators will be interested in the morale, energy, and big picture involved in the issue being discussed. Communicators who are using a people focus will be more interested in getting to know you; small talk is important before diving into a meeting agenda or doing business.

In a meeting this may sound like:

"What are the benefits of this proposal to the employees who will be affected by the changes we are initiating? Who will be most affected? How could we include them in the planning of this project?"

"What are you feeling about this? Do you have a gut instinct for this?

"How can we influence our Japanese counterparts to see this in the same way we do? Currently they are viewing the industry needs differently from the way we do, and we need to understand why."

By answering these two questions—is the person extroverted or introverted, and is the person task-focused or people-focused—you will be able to identify the preferred communication style for the moment. You will be able to have a conversation that addresses the specific needs of someone else's style. My goal is to show you how to do this at any time. My goal is NOT to have you put people in boxes and leave them there—people's communication needs will change, based on the situation they are in. It is important that you see what is happening in the moment, so you can guide the conversation in a way that builds trust and rapport instead of tension.

Outgoing/extroverted, task-oriented communication is a sign that the Dominant Communication Style is in play.

Outgoing/extroverted, people-oriented communication is a sign that the Influence Communication Style is in play.

Internal/introverted, people-oriented communication is a sign that the Steady Communication Style is in play.

Internal/introverted, task-oriented communication is a sign that the Compliant-to-Standards Communication Style is in play.

So what does this really mean? There are predictable communication needs that emerge from each style. The most effective way to gain the commitment and cooperation of others is to provide what they need, to understand their styles, and to blend your own so that you connect with them. By identifying another person or group's communication needs, you can adapt to that style and gain the person or group's attention.

Let's look at each of the four pure styles in depth.

## Dominant Style Communication Patterns

People with the Dominant style preference need the following:

Activity

Opportunity to respond to problems and debate

Challenges

Power

Quick decision making and a willingness to remake decisions as they acquire more information

Variety and lots of change

Opportunity to be a self-starter

Results

New ideas and new and unique products to buy

Those with other styles describe Dominant behavior in these ways:

Bold

Demanding

Pioneering

Aggressive

Driving

Competitive

Ambitious

Curious

Responsible

Relying on gut instincts

Juggling too many activities

Rushing with a strong sense of urgency to get things done

Willing to break the rules to be more efficient

People with this style will fight back when they experience external conflict. They need to learn that those with other styles are not as direct with their feelings as they are. High Dominant communicators also love to make quick decisions, but they often do not realize that those with other styles cannot do this. They will interrupt others whom they perceive to be too slow. Their sense of urgency to make a decision is often what creates conflict. Instead they need to give others a few days to think and prepare for a discussion. On the phone they prefer to get right to the point, with little to no chitchat.

The Dominant style communicator adds value to a team in the following ways:

Innovation

Initiation of activity

Making decisions quickly in a crisis

Being challenge-oriented or argumentative

Placing a high value on managing time efficiently

Being a bottom-line organizer

Tenacity

Challenging the status quo

Competitiveness

Paying attention to the big picture and the concept or vision

Taking risks that those with other styles will not be willing to take

The Dominant style communicator wants these workplace elements:

Forums for verbalizing his or her ideas

Quick decisions

Prestige, position, and powerful titles

Ways to demonstrate success

Power and authority to achieve results

Control of his or her own destiny and opportunities to lead others

Projects that are well suited to the Dominant Communication Style include:

Freedom from controls and direct supervision

Nonroutine work that includes risk, challenges, and new opportunities

Evaluation based on the results produced, not how the process was done

A forum to express ideas and suggestions efficiently

Lots of activity and movement

When communicating with people showing Dominant style patterns, do these things:

Stick to business.

Be clear and to the point.

Ask questions that begin with the word "What."

Present facts logically and plan your presentation in advance.

Take issue with the facts directly in a disagreement; be bold and confident.

Have a well-organized package; look professional and polished.

Make decisions quickly, knowing that you can re-make the decision later, if additional facts arise that warrant reviewing the decision.

Some public figures who use the Dominant style as their predominant communication behavior include:

Donald Trump

Hillary Clinton

Steve Jobs

Mark Zuckerberg

Serena Williams

Nancy Pelosi

Captain Kirk (*Star Trek*)

Lee Iacocca

Jack Welch

Simon Cowell (*American Idol*)

Robert Irvine (*Restaurant: Impossible*)

Dwight Schrute (*The Office*)

Michael Jordan

High Dominant communicators will be direct and to the point. To those with other communication styles they will appear blunt, argumentative, and overly results-focused. After a heated debate, people with this communication style do not hold a grudge, and they may not realize that some with other styles do. Prose and flowery language may turn them off.

Each style has limitations or blind spots. It is important to know the Dominant style limitations:

They may lack tact and diplomacy in selling new ideas and suggestions; they can appear bossy.

They take on too much, too soon, too fast.

They focus too heavily on tasks that get results and avoid building relationships.

They refuse to listen to people considered to be less experienced or competent.

They push or bully people, instead of leading them.

They are overly argumentative and appear not to be listening.

They are impatient pushing for decisions or action now.

They will overstep their authority if they do not understand where the boundaries are.

## Influence Style Communication Patterns

People with the Influence style preference need the following:

To interact socially with others

Activity

A favorable environment

Opportunities for fun

Opportunity to sell their ideas and influence others to their points of view

To be liked, to hear affirmations

Emotional connection to others—talking about feelings

Influence style behavior can be seen as:

Enthusiastic

Inspiring

Magnetic

Political

Persuasive

Warm

Charming

Polished

Trusting

Sociable

Poised

Quick to decide—may appear impulsive in buying what they want

Emotional

Optimistic

Talkative—chatty

People with this style may verbally lash out or fight and then run when they feel conflict. They can be seen by those with other styles as being verbally intense or abusive when angry.

They will interrupt others because they are so chatty and full of ideas. They do not mean their interruptions to squash others; they are simply feeling excited about what they are discussing.

On the phone they may initiate long conversations and will have a great deal of tone variation in their voices as they chit-chat about all the events of their day and their thoughts on everything.

These are huggers; they will greet you with a warm hug, even if they are new acquaintances. They warmly touch your arm to confirm agreement.

The Influence style communicator adds value to a team in the following ways:

Verbalizing thinking clearly

Ease with words

Positive sense of humor

Motivating others toward goals and to be part of the team

Negotiating or facilitating when there is conflict on the team

Building morale and creating hope for new possibilities with their warm, friendly, fun demeanor

Those with the Influence style want these workplace elements:

People who appreciate their verbal conversational abilities

Social recognition—public acknowledgment of what they are doing

Variety of people to connect with and build connections with

Identification with a team or group—time to socialize with the group members

Freedom of speech and lots of people to speak with daily

Positive, uplifting, optimistic people to interact with

Group activities—teams to belong to outside the work environment

Warm connections to others

Projects that are well suited to those with the Influence Communication Style include the following:

Activities that involve working with teams—lots of people to interact with

Freedom to move around easily

A manager who appreciates that they share their thinking and feelings easily

Optimistic work culture that appreciates their warm, friendly, fun style

Work tasks that change frequently—they love variety

Assignments that involve inspiring, connecting, and networking with other people

Freedom from detail

When communicating with people showing Influence style patterns, do these things:

Show that you are open to interacting—ask friendly, warm questions to engage.

Be stimulating and fast moving.

Use emotion and inspiring language.

Ask questions about their goals, dreams, and aspirations.

Ask their opinions on ideas you are considering.

Be optimistic and forward-looking.

Express your emotion freely, and ask about how they are feeling.

Listen, showing direct eye contact, when they express their feelings.

Be direct, and share your creative ideas.

Appreciate their trusting nature.

Understand they can be quick decision makers wanting the showy new products.

Provide ideas and structures that will bring their creative ideas alive.

Provide testimonials from people they see as important.

Offer incentives for their willingness to take risks.

Some public figures who use the Influence style as their predominant communication pattern include:

Former President Ronald Reagan

Oprah Winfrey

Bill and Giuliana Rancic

George Stephanopoulos

Shelly Lazarus

Lady Gaga

Katy Perry

Jim Carrey

Ellen DeGeneres

Jay Leno

Bill Cosby

Former President Bill Clinton

Companies like Zappos, Disney, Southwest Airlines, and Ben & Jerry's, which strive to make business look fun, are exhibiting the High Influence tendency. Whom do you know who frequently uses this communication style?

High Influence conversation will be wordy, flowery, emotional, charming, outgoing, fun.

Each style has limitations or blind spots. It is important to know the Influence style limitations:

They need help in creating structures and organization.

They need focus to help them stay on track with their goals, as they can be easily distracted.

They have a tendency to interrupt others because they have so much they want to say.

They lash out at others when they are upset, which may seem verbally abusive to others.

## Steady Style Communication Patterns

People with the Steady style preference need the following:

Established standards and methods

A stable and predictable environment

Personal attention and recognition for ongoing commitment to the project and for tasks completed consistently

An environment where long-standing relationships can be developed

An environment that gives time to adjust to changes

Steady behavior can be seen in these ways:

Mild

Friendly

Systematic

Sincere

Nondemonstrative

Team-playing

Patient

Stable

Kind

Understanding

Predictable

Amiable

Passive compared to other styles

People with this style of communication will put up with what is being asked of them when they feel conflict. They do not want to argue; it is uncomfortable for them to stand up to someone else in a conversation. Later, they may feel resentful that they were pushed to do something they did not want to do. They can hold onto bitterness and resentment at someone for a very long time without openly admitting that they feel this way. Great listeners, they will not interrupt others. On the phone, they are warm conversationalists, friendly and concerned for the other person or team.

The Steady style communicator adds value to a team in the following ways:

Patience for all

Logical, step-by-step thinker

Great listener

Creating an easygoing, relaxed culture

Dependable team worker

Finishing tasks committed to

Reconciling, calming, and stabilizing other team members

The Steady style communicator needs these workplace elements:

To serve

Patient, relaxed conversations and relationships

Loyalty

Long-term projects and relationships

Closure on projects and decisions before starting something new

To work for a leader with a cause

A favorable—no conflict—environment

A steady pace that allows time to consider options before making decisions

Time to make decisions

Little variety in day-to-day activity

Projects that are well suited to those with the Steady Communication style include:

Completing work that has a clear step-by-step model already established

Long-term assignments

Working with the same team members for long periods of time

When communicating with people showing Steady style patterns, do these things:

Move casually and informally; begin with personal comments to break the ice.

Ask about their families and personal lives. It is for their families and their causes that they do what they are doing, so respect that this is what is most important to them.

Ask "How" questions.

Present your case logically, nonthreateningly, giving time for them to digest and ask questions.

Provide personal assurances and guarantees.

Patiently draw out their goals and ideas.

Listen and be responsive to what they say. Show you are contemplating their input and explain how you are going to (or not going to) move forward with their ideas and why.

Allow them at least three days to think and weigh the options when making decisions.

Don't mistake their willingness to go along for agreement or satisfaction. Look for signs that they may have hurt feelings, because they will often not express these directly, and it will be important to uncover them so that resentment does not bubble up later.

Some public figures who use the Steady style as their predominant communication pattern include:

Mother Teresa

Former President, George H. W. Bush

Former First Lady Laura Bush

Warren Buffett

Ken Chenault (CEO American Express)

Ram Charan (author of *Execution*)

Martin Luther King, Jr.

Queen Elizabeth II

Mohandas Gandhi

Fred Rogers (TV host from *Mr. Rogers' Neighborhood*)

Tom Brokaw

Whom do you know who frequently uses this communication style?

High Steady conversation can be characterized in these ways:

Introverted

People focused

Indirect

Focused on stability

Slow decision making spread over days or weeks in several conversations

Relaxed, with no sense of urgency (even if there is urgency)

Each style has limitations or blind spots. It is important to know the High Steady style communicators' limitations:

They lack emotion. It may be hard to read their feelings; they often do not themselves know what they are feeling about something until they are asked to explore it.

They are possessive.

They appear in agreement or support for an idea because they are uncomfortable working through conflict.

They need preparation and time to adjust to changing circumstances.

They have homey clutter around them.

They take constructive criticism of their work as a personal affront, so it can be hard to give them feedback to help them grow.

They need help getting started on something new, because they like to do what is tried and trusted, rather than start new, unknown projects.

They internalize their feelings; they tend not to discuss their hurt feelings to gain resolution and move on.

They wait for orders or direction from others before taking action; they need someone to tell them what to do, because they may not take initiative on their own.

They stay involved in a situation that is not good for them, because they do not project a sense of urgency.

They are stubborn, locked into their ways of thinking about or doing something

The High Steady style communicator can be seen as:

Relaxed

Predictable

Stable

Reliable

Deliberate

Consistent

Nondemonstrative, not into drama

Resistant to change

## Compliant-to-Standards Style Communication Patterns

People with the Compliant-to-Standards style preference need the following:

Direct and to-the-point conversations

Fact-based conversations

Logic

Proven results

Guarantees

Rules

Low risks and the ability to collect information about pros and cons before decisions are made

No impulsive actions

No emotionalized dramatic communication

Compliant-to-Standards behavior can be seen in these ways:

Accurate

Mature

Conscientious

Fact-focused

Systematic

Analytical

Methodical

Exacting

Restrained

Precise

Diplomatic

Patient

Unemotional or fear-based

People with this style of communication will avoid dealing with the issue when they feel conflict; they need to learn how to address and negotiate differences in opinions and feelings early on before they turn into deep conflict. This does not come easily for them, because it is about subjective emotion and they prefer to deal in facts and logic. They will not interrupt others unless they are pushed to the edge and feel intense anger. On the phone, they get right to the point, with little or no chit-chat: "Just the facts, ma'am."

The Compliant-to-Standards communicator adds value to a team in the following ways:

Conscientiousness

Defining, clarifying, getting information, criticizing, and testing fact-based thinking

Objective thinking

Maintaining high standards and quality controls

Being task focused

Asking lots of questions

Being diplomatic

Paying attention to small details and the next task at hand to implement the desired result

High quality and safety standards

Perfectionism, double checking all details

Those with the Compliant-to-Standards style want these workplace elements:

Procedures

Manuals

Precision and attention to details

Proof and evidence

Doing work by the book

Safe environments

Quality controls

Projects that are well suited for those with the Compliant-to-Standards Communication Style include:

Quality control implementation and procedures

Technical, task-oriented work in deeply specialized areas

Assignments that can be followed through to completion

Tasks where critical thinking is needed and rewarded

Minimal noise and people distractions or interruptions

Little need for customer service or bedside manner

When communicating with people showing Compliant-to-Standards style patterns, do these things:

Speak in fact-based language, not emotions.

Be direct and to the point—be all business—let them decide whether they want to socialize after the work is done.

Prepare your case in advance; give them a detailed agenda, so they can prepare ahead of time.

Be formal.

Build credibility by showing that you have looked at all sides of the issue.

Present specifics and do exactly what you say you will do.

Create a proposed action plan with a time line and milestones—a spreadsheet that shows the whole project plan—and ask for their input.

Do not be abrupt or rapid in your speaking.

Be prepared to answer loads of questions.

Give them time to make decisions based on what they want. It will take at least three days for them to digest the information, so ask, "When would you like to review this again? I'm available to answer your questions, and here is how you can reach me over the next few days."

Use data and facts to disagree—no emotional appeals.

Shake their hands and look them in the eye, and then do not touch them again. These are not huggy-touchy-mushy types; they do not like public displays of affection.

Some public figures with the Compliant-to-Standards style as their predominant communication pattern include:

Allen Greenspan

Bill Gates

Al Gore

Donald Rumsfeld

Sherlock Holmes

Tiger Woods

Mr. Spock (*Star Trek*)

Diane Sawyer

Courtney Cox (character on *Friends* TV show)

Meryl Streep

Barbara Walters

Jack Nicklaus

Whom do you know who frequently uses this communication style?

High Compliant-to-Standards conversation will be:

Introverted

Task focused

Direct

Focused on avoiding problems—risk mitigation

Each style has limitations or blind spots. It is important to know the Compliant-to-Standards style communicator's limitations:

They are too critical of themselves and others

They are unaware of how often they squash others emotionally; they need to develop self-awareness and empathy for other's feelings to keep other people engaged with them.

They have the most difficulty with High Influencers who want to express emotions and seem too impulsive.

35

They have difficulty with High Dominant communicators who seem fixed in their own points of view and want to make decisions quickly, based on the first evidence they find that supports their points of view.

## What Is the Right Style?

There is not one right style. Right and wrong are judgments that relate to ethics. We are not talking about ethics here. We are focused on understanding people's communication needs. The issue is what you do with *your* communication style to be effective when collaborating with others.

Each style has predictable strengths and blind spots, and when you understand how these play together, you will begin to collaborate with people to play to their strengths and to cover their blind spots. You will no longer take it personally or be offended when you bump up against someone's blind spots. It is not personal when someone who has a High Compliant-to-Standards Communication Style does not greet you with a warm hug. Likewise, when someone gives you a big warm hug the first time he sees you, you'll recognize a clue that points to the Influence communication pattern.

I advise my coaching clients to look at their "That's for Me!" list, and to look at each project and ask, "Who will be able to collaborate with me based on his or her strengths?" Begin to give detailed, analytical, research projects to people who are comfortable with the Compliant-to-Standards window. Give projects that require lots of people interaction in exploring new ideas to those who are comfortable with the Influence Communication Style. Give projects that involve following established processes, executing the same pattern over and over, to someone comfortable with the Steady Communication Style. Give assignments that are focused on change, challenge, the big picture, testing boundaries, and high risk to someone who is comfortable with the Dominant Communication Style. Design projects and roles in your workplace that are doable based on the communication style needs of the work being done.

Some professions and the communication style tendencies drawn to that work:

Trial attorneys: *Dominant*

Chief executive officers: *Dominant*

Outside sales representatives: *Influence*

Community affairs and public relations: *Influence*

Advertising: *Influence*

Route sales: *Steady*

Nurses: *Steady*

Elementary-school Teachers: *Steady*

Manufacturing line work: *Steady*

Accountants: *Compliant*

Dentists: *Compliant*

Engineering: *Compliant*

Professional trainers and speakers: *Dominant + Influence*

Commission sales: *Dominant + Influence*

Customer service: *Steady + Influence*

Emergency room doctors: *Dominant + Compliant*

Surgeons: *Dominant + Compliant*

Understanding communication styles not only helps you bring out the best in your employees by connecting them with projects suited to their modes of operating, it can also help you fine-tune your ability to persuade and influence customers, investors, or anyone with whom you need to share your vision.

If you know your audience well, it's much easier to tailor the delivery and content of your message to make it more effective.

Peter Guber is the chairman and CEO of Mandalay Entertainment. The films he has produced include *Rain Man, Batman, The Color Purple, Midnight Express, Gorillas in the Mist: The Story of Dian Fossey, The Witches of Eastwick, Missing,* and *Flashdance.* Guber's films have earned over $3 billion worldwide and 50 Academy Award nominations. Clearly he knows how to get results. Guber said: "A great storyteller never tells a story the same way twice. Instead, she sees what is unique in each storytelling experience and responds fully to what is demanded. A story involving your company should sound different each time. Whether you tell it to 2,000 customers at a convention, 500 salespeople at a marketing meeting, ten stock analysts in a conference call, or three CEOs over drinks, tailor it to the situation. . . . Great storytellers prepare obsessively. They think about, rethink, work, and rework their stories to fit the audience."

What does it take to do what Guber suggests? Know how to people read your audience. Know how to identify what their needs are, so you meet their needs in your presentations and conversations. When you know how to do this, you will experience a new level of confidence in your ability to connect meaningfully as you engage with people.

Know your story so well that you can tailor it to the situation you are in, like a jazz musician who can improvise on a riff while he matches the harmony with others. Know how to read your audience as well. Then you will be able to tailor your story to the people in front of you for them to hear your message in a way that is engaging to them.

I have described the four "pure" communication styles. Most of us prefer a combination of these four styles. Research done by a company I collaborate with, Target Training International, revealed these insights:

19 percent of the population prefers a style that has Dominant as the highest preference.

32 percent of the population prefers a style that has Influence as the highest preference.

35 percent of the population prefers a style that has Steady as the highest preference.

14 percent of the population prefers a style that has Compliant as the highest preference


2 percent of the population prefers the pure Dominant style

1 percent of the population prefers the pure Influence style

1 percent of the population prefers the pure Steady style

1 percent of the population prefers the pure Compliant-to–Standards style

How do these numbers affect your approach to mastering communication styles? First, learn how to adapt to each of the pure styles, and then practice identifying the combination patterns, beginning with the Steady style. For example, how will a person who prefers the Steady and Compliant-to-Standards communication patterns show up in a meeting? Then how will a person who prefers the Steady and Influence patterns show up? What will someone who prefers the Influence/Dominant combination pattern want to focus on in a conversation? Practice creating conversations that will appeal to each of these combinations.

It is not possible to be all things to all people. I am not suggesting that you need to be able to turn yourself inside out to build deep rapport with every person you meet.

If using this information about communication styles is not about trying to be all things to all people, what is it about? It's about guiding yourself and others toward the right roles and assignments on a team or in a workplace; it's about speaking to people in a way that they can hear you; it's about valuing differences and knowing how to bring out the best in others. Your ability to adapt your behavior and conversations to each of the styles will increase your effectiveness in communication and enable greater understanding and appreciation of others' similarities and differences.

> *"To avoid criticism, do nothing, say nothing, be nothing."*
> —Elbert Hubbard

## Tamara's Story

Although Tamara has been working in her job for five years, she now wants new results at work. Tamara's preferred communication style is High Compliant-to-Standards, with a Steady style as back up. Tamara has a Low Dominant communication drive.

She is now ready to climb out of a rut she has been in for too long. Tamara is a supervisor who feels her boss is not hearing her. Her inability to communicate effectively with her boss has affected her relationships at work. Because of this, she has to guard against having a "no one hears me," victim thought pattern when working with her team. As a result of what she has learned about people reading, Tamara is ready to make some big changes, so that she can create a community of positive collaboration around her instead of the rut-stuck state she has been living in. Would you like to know how Tamara lifted herself out of this victim story and began to be a hero in her organization?

For a long time Tamara expected other people, including her boss, to use her communication style when working with her. Tamara was not adapting her communication to others' needs.

When we began to talk about the communication style patterns, Tamara was able to see immediately that her boss's pattern was the opposite of hers. In other words, Tamara's boss prefers a High Influence Communication Style with a Dominant backup. These styles are directly across the wheel from each other.

We have the most difficulty understanding the communication from people who are opposite us on the "Success Insights Wheel," Figure 2.1. Our communication patterns—the wiring of our brains—is very different.

Tamara has been taking it personally when her boss does not respond as she thinks he should. She has assumed negative intent from him, based on their style differences. In order to overcome her own bitterness and stuck-in-a-victim-rut thought pattern, Tamara had to understand her boss from his perspective. She began to think about how he needed information. Because he has a High Influence style with a Dominant backup, he likes a fast pace, wants the big picture first with a clear request, instead of lots of details building up to a request after several conversations. He wants to make decisions quickly and is open to changing his mind frequently; he likes to know who is aligned with whom and wants more friendly interaction. He even appreciates an emotional appeal for action, because he wants to be inspired. Instead Tamara has been very tight-lipped, aloof, and distant with him. She has presented facts, data, and logic intending to build a case over time, leading him to see all the research she has done and how that led her to certain conclusions. He does not think like this. He has seen her as being in the weeds, too analytical, and much too distant for him to align with her.

Since Tamara is the one who wants change in their relationship, she is the one who needs to adapt to his preferred communication style. No matter your role, whether you are peer, employee, or boss, if you are the one who wants change in a relationship, it is your job to adapt to the other person's communication style.

When Tamara began to adapt her communication style, she experienced new results with her boss. She also began to look at what communication styles others were using in their conversations. She began to realize that she needed to use the Dominant Communication Style when she was faced with challenges and problems that needed quick decisions. She would ask peers and colleagues who had this style and could help her think this way when she was faced with these challenges.

Tamara also realized that it was better to use the Influence Communication Style when thinking about selling ideas, engaging others in getting results, or wanting to inspire engagement. If a team needed to think about how work would be done, then using the Steady Communication Style made sense. When logic, research, problem solving, and procedures were needed, the Compliant-to-Standards window was helpful.

Tamara became masterful in recognizing the communication needs of the moment. She began to help others in her organization to understand the communication styles and to solve complex people issues that had been causing problems across departments for some time. Tamara decided to earn the certification to debrief people in their assessment reports for her organization. Tamara's reputation in her organization changed dramatically in less than a year, because of the dramatic growth in her ability to connect with people in new ways.

Your communication style falls within the wheel shown in Figure 2.1.

## What to Do with Discussion Styles

### The Dominant style is looking for RESULTS

- Be confident.
- Close, take action.
- Disagree with facts, not people.
- Focus on issues.

- Use emphatic hand gestures.
- Do not be overpowered by them.
- Let them win (you win too).
- Move faster than normal.
- Match their intensity and strength, but stay friendly.

**FIGURE 2.1 THE SUCCESS INSIGHTS WHEEL™**

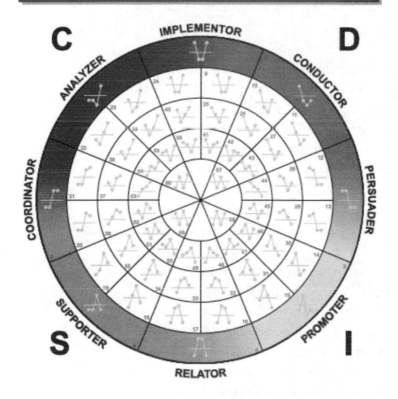

Copyright © 1992–2005, Target Training International, Ltd. All rights reserved.

### The Influence style is looking for the EXPERIENCE

- Allow them to talk, but keep focus, and keep asking questions focused on topic.
- Minimize interest in details of topic.
- Focus on the forest, not the trees.
- Provide structure and steps, ensure they have something to follow up on.
- Give recognition.
- Listen to their stories.
- Have fun with them.
- "Jump" to close during high-energy moments.
- Stay positive, upbeat, high energy.

### The Steady style is looking for SECURITY

- Tell them *how* something will be done.
- Provide the reassurances they need.
- Be yourself—relaxed, authentic, casual.
- Take action when you feel you have their trust.
- Assure them they made the right decision.
- Introduce them to others; help them build relationships.
- Show them your follow-up after action.
- Give them the facts and the step-by-step actions.

### The Compliant style is looking for INFORMATION

- Answer questions with facts and logic.
- Don't be too personal.
- Be direct and friendly.
- Do not hug or stand too close.
- Be professional, not too relaxed.
- Expect skepticism.
- Follow through on details.
- Give information and then close; close when they say they are ready.

On a photo shoot one day, working with a professional photographer, I noticed him taking pictures with three or four different cameras. I asked him why, and he explained that they have different lenses. Each camera takes a photo that is different from the others. Even though the cameras are taking photos of the same subject, the end products look different. One camera has a wide-angle lens, another has a colored lens, and another can zoom in on small details. The photographer's explanation reminded me of what happens when a person begins to understand each of the communication styles; he or she has better tools (more lenses) for achieving better results. Like this photographer, who could now produce photos from different lenses, a person who understands and uses the communication style model will be able to create broader, more comprehensive conversations and outcomes.

Have you noticed that two people can see the exact same thing and describe it very differently? Have you ever been in a situation where you did something and then someone else gave you feedback that was not at all like you imagined your behavior?

Until we are trained to be observers—to use the various lenses available to us—we simply do not see ourselves the way we show up to others. If you learn and master this skill, you will raise your awareness of the range of behaviors that are possible and effective in conversations.

## How People Learn Based on Communication Styles

There are four basic learning styles.

### Style One: The Dominant Communication Style

People who prefer the Dominant Communication Style prefer to learn independently by doing, rather than by reflecting and thinking things through step-by-step. They enjoy taking charge of their learning agendas, and they want to focus intensely so they make the most of their time. They may appear bored or impatient in workshops and seminars, because they prefer to learn by trial and error as they are producing results. They want to learn the hot, new, trendy skill or behavior, and they are quick to try the latest new tool. They enjoy change, so they embrace learning to create new results.

### Style Two: The Influence Communication Style
People who prefer the Influence Communication Style prefer to learn by doing with others in groups. They enjoy attending seminars and workshops and being mentored by people in and out of the organization. These people will likely resist taking an on-line course alone, because they want someone to verbalize what they are learning, and they also want to have an opportunity to learn via social interaction.

### Style Three: The Steady Communication Style
People who prefer the Steady Communication Style appreciate opportunities to learn that provide time for reflecting on experiences and thinking things out step-by-step. These people appreciate hand-holding through each step; they want to watch you do the step, then do it themselves with you watching, and then do it again to get your feedback. They appear to be slower learners, however the benefit of their style is that they will stick with what they are learning for a long time once they do learn a new skill or behavior. Although they are slower learners, they learn the new skill thoroughly and will use it longer than High Dominants or Influences will.

### Style Four: The Compliant-to-Standards Communication Style
People who prefer the Compliant-to-Standards Communication Style appreciate systems that encourage independent thinking. They appreciate self-study, on-line learning that is highly structured with study guides and certification exams. They like to have training and policy manuals for the work they are doing.

They also like formal higher education programs such as master's degrees and rigorous certifications.

## Predictable Patterns That Sabotage Effective Collaboration

There are several predictable patterns that show up when people who are not aware of communication styles interact with each other.

### The Steady and Dominant Together

When a person with a High Dominant style interacts with a person with a High Steady style, and they are not trained in this model, the dance patterns between them are predictable. We have a fast decision maker with a slow decision maker.

The Steady style communicator will describe the Dominant style communicator in the following ways:

A bully, who overpowers everyone

Too intense and fast paced—everything is urgent—he has fire drills every day

Taking too many risks and creating change for the sake of change

Addicted to making decisions—will make a decision on Tuesday saying, "This is what we are doing! Make ABC happen," and then will come back the following week, re-make the decision, or worse say, "Where is DFG? I asked for DFG last week! You all are not focused on the right things!"

Not listening

Only focused on the big picture and overcommitting what the team is capable of doing

Too task focused—never asks how I am doing or how my family is

Overfocused on creating challenges and change

The Dominant style communicator will describe the Steady style communicator in the following ways:

Too slow—nothing seems to be getting done on an effective time line

Showing no sense of urgency

Focused on how things will be done before we even agree about what we are doing

Too soft—always talking about family, personal stuff, and not focusing enough on the task at hand

Going along with whatever I say—a pushover who does not have a backbone or share thinking

Nonemotional—I can't tell if he wants to be on the team or not

Overfocused on security

Even though one has an extroverted, task-focused style and is interacting with someone who has an introverted, people-focused style, these two can become an incredible team if they play to each other's strengths and cover each other's blind spots. For this combination to succeed, the High Dominant communicator (High D) will need to slow down and build trust. Before diving into work, he needs to ask, "How are you doing? Did you have an enjoyable weekend?" and listen to her answer. She will need time to make decisions. Give her as much information as possible several days before the meeting in which he intends to make decisions. The High D needs to realize that lack of emotional display does not mean that she agrees. The

High D needs to not just listen to words but also observe body language and facial expressions. The High Steady (High S) needs to be bold and ask directly for what she wants, not assume he should know this already, not wonder why he is not giving her what she wants. High Ds respect communication that is direct, straightforward, and focused on the goals and task that will produce results. The High S must stand up to the High D to grow in their relationship. She can use a series of questions to have the High D explain himself and defend his thinking.

### The Influence and Compliant-to-Standards Styles Together

When a person with a High Influence style and a person with a High Compliant-to-Standards style interact, and they are not trained in this model, these common dynamics play out in a predictable dance. This is a person with an extroverted, trusting, optimistic style and a person with an introverted, non-trusting, pessimistic style. Here again we have a slow decision maker and a fast decision maker, which is very challenging for both people in this dynamic.

The Compliant-to-Standards style communicator will describe the High Influence style communicator as:

Too emotional and extroverted

Too loose with the facts—not sure I trust what he is saying

Taking unnecessary risks

Communicating too much—how do I get her to stop talking all the time? She says the same thing over and over again!

The High Influence style communicator will see the Compliant-to-Standards style communicator as:

Too analytical—focused only on facts, logic, and data— only seeing the trees and not the forest

Not fun, playful, or creative—taking the fun out of everything

Nerdy

Risk-averse and afraid of everything—can be downright negative

Not communicating enough—how can I get him to share what he is feeling? I try so hard to draw him out, but he is a cold fish!

These are two different lenses that could not be more opposite! For this combination to work, the High Influencer (High I) will need to slow down, keep a tight rein on her emotions, show up on time, and structure her work in a logical A-to-Z framework in order to connect with the High Compliant (High C). She will need to begin with data and facts. She should not expect personal, social conversation, as that would be considered private to the High C individual. The High C will need to realize the High I is not lying when she does not have the facts right; facts are not her area of focus. High I is more interested in the emotional connection and the quality of the relationships with the people in the meeting. This is an unknown experience for the High C. The High C will need to loosen up and intentionally express more interest in people and having fun. The High C will be more effective if he picks up his pace, asks supportive questions that keep the High I focused, and is patient with the High I's need to verbalize what she is doing. She is a verbal processor and must say it to know what she is thinking. They can become an incredible team, if they play to each other's strengths and cover each other's blind spots.

## How You Can Benefit from Feedback

Often I work with an executive and his or her team. The executive wants to know how her team, peers, manager, leaders, and clients perceive working with her. She may have received feedback from someone that implies she does not seem to be aware of how others experience working with her, and now she wants to know the objective truth. She may want to continue to improve her ability to build relationships and collaborate with new teams. In some cases she realizes she needs to change how she is perceived in order for her to grow to the next level. This is usually the moment when an executive reaches out to me to provide her with a 360 survey. To do this, I speak with numerous people whom she selects. I individually ask this group of people lots of questions about what it is like to work with her. After having done hundreds of these 360 surveys, it is clear there are typical patterns that emerge. The feedback, when viewed through the lens of communication styles, becomes clearer, and it's also easier to design a professional development plan for moving forward. I'm going to share the two most common feedback reports with you so you can see what they look like. See if you can you spot the communication styles described in the following 360 survey reports.

## Sophia's 360 Survey

Sophia is a vice president who would like to be promoted to president in her global organization. Here are Sophia's 360 Survey key themes, summarized from 12 conversations with her team members, peers, bosses, and clients.

### Strengths—Sophia:

Sophia is competent—she knows the business better than anyone.

She is results oriented, always focused on creating new solutions to difficult challenges.

She thinks faster than anyone in the room.

She makes decisions for herself and for her team very quickly.

She is confident and to the point in her speaking with others.

She consistently produces results.

She comes to meetings prepared with an agenda and knows what she wants from each person.

She is highly responsive to requests from others.

She likes to win and wants to create winning teams.

### What would you like to see *more* of from Sophia?

Listen—don't interrupt, use body language that says you are sincerely interested in what others have to say.

Ask questions because you are curious and want to learn from others—even those below your level.

Be patient with others in group settings.

Let other people shine sometimes—the limelight does not always need to be on you.

Be aware about when to be transactional versus when to be more strategic.

Communicate the big picture more often so we know why we are doing what you are asking.

Collaborate—work with people, don't just tell them what to do.

Be more consultative.

Be open to socializing, not just focused on business all the time.

Share your experiences with team members, so they can learn from you.

Acknowledge the accomplishments of others.

### What would you like to see *less* of from Sophia?

Arrogance—she thinks that only she has the right answer.

Harsh, prickly, abrasive communication

Bravado

Obvious focus on the level of the person who is speaking

Name-dropping the high-level people that she knows well.

Not trying to prove that she knows everything and that she can solve it all herself—she is always striving and it is hard to be relaxed with her.

Overselling—she toots her own horn so much.

Using all capitals, bold, red, underlined content in e-mails.

Listening to defend her own thinking—it is obvious from her body language that she has formed her opinion from the first third of my paragraph and she has not heard where I am going with my point, but she is ready to jump in to speak.

### What else would be helpful for me to know about working with Sophia?

I'm glad I am on her good side, because I would not want to be on her bad side.

I'm worried she may think I pointed out her faults in the feedback report, and she will then come on the attack. I do not want to lose my job. I'm afraid of her.

I wish Sophia would not try so hard to show people how capable she is and instead show how amazing her team members and peers are; that is what will take her to the next level.

Some people are afraid to engage with her, because they are uncomfortable with the conflict she will create; she loves a challenge, but not everyone does, and she does not seem to realize how this affects group dynamics around her.

She is so intense I have to prepare to meet with her.

Based on this 360 survey, what is Sophia's communication style? How is this affecting her ability to grow to the next level? What recommendations would you make if Sophia reported to you? If Sophia were your boss, how would you approach communicating with her?

## Bob's 360 Survey

Bob has been in a director role for the past five years. He knows the vice president position will be opening in a few months, because the person in that role has announced he is retiring. Bob wants to know from his 360 survey how others perceive him, so he is prepared to discuss what it will take for him to be considered for the VP role. Here are Bob's 360 Survey key themes, summarized from 10 conversations with his team members, peers, and bosses.

**Strengths—Bob:**

Bob works tirelessly.

He listens well and incorporates what others say into his work.

He will follow up on every detail.

He is tenacious and will persevere.

Bob has long-term relationships with people.

He invests more time in projects than anyone else.

He is always approachable and friendly.

He is so easy to talk to that sometimes I forget I am talking to my boss.

He is task-oriented and gets the job done by working long hours.

He is eager to please others.

He is loyal and I trust him.

**What would you like to see more of from Bob?**

Be more proactive—currently he is too reactive.

Prioritize the work that needs to be done, and align it to the strategic plan.

Assert your ideas more directly, instead of waiting to be asked.

Be a leader—he often appears to be subservient to others, or too hands-off with his team.

Promote your abilities more directly.

Show enthusiasm and energy for the project we are working on.

Show some emotion—does he want to be engaged in what we are doing? It is not obvious.

Be decisive and confident in your decision-making.

Create agendas and take charge of meetings; plot a course and take a stand for the direction of the team; don't wait for someone else to tell you what to do.

Use formal communication that looks like it was planned with forethought.

Delegate to others and don't be afraid of dealing with the performance issues on the team.

Give group presentations (instead of one-at-time conversations with lots of people).

### What would you like to see less of from Bob?

Conflict avoidance—Bob does not like conflict in any form, and this is a big problem because he has blinders on about some issues that need attention.

Talking about people behind their backs—as the boss, he should be dealing with the issues, not making them worse by pointing out people's weaknesses to others.

Last-minute requests—they are a sign he forgot to plan for something and is now in reactive mode.

**What else would be helpful for me to know about working with Bob?**

When I get upset, angry or hurt, that is when I get his attention; otherwise he does not act like things are urgent. I often wonder what needs to exist for him to engage without me needing to get upset.

Based on this 360 feedback, what is Bob's communication style? How is this affecting his ability to grow to the next level? What recommendations would you make, if Bob reported to you? If Bob were your boss, how would you approach communicating with him?

When you understand how to blend your own style and play to the strengths of others' styles, you will experience improved communication, more effective conversations, and deeper relationships, which generate both trust and results.

## People Reading: Preferred Communication Styles Application Exercise

Whom do you know that prefers the Dominant style?

What can you do to adapt your style to be effective when collaborating with Dominant style communicators?

Identify someone you know with whom you can practice creating conversations to build rapport so you are ready when you see this style in action.

Identify which items on your "That's for Me!" list will require the Dominant Communication Style.

Whom do you know who prefers the Influence style?

What can you do to adapt your style to be effective when collaborating with Influence style communicators?

Identify which items on your "That's for Me!" list will require the Influence Communication Style. This style would be useful in the following situations: introducing yourself to people you do not know; inviting others to a meeting, party, or event; building diverse relationships across an industry or organization; and brainstorming creative ideas with a group in a conversation for exploring new possibilities.

Whom do you know who prefers the Steady Communication Style?

What can you do to adapt your style to be effective when collaborating with Steady style communicators?

Identify which items on your "That's for Me!" list will require the Steady Communication style.

Whom do you know who prefers the Compliant-to-Standards style?

What can you do to adapt your style to be effective when collaborating with Compliant-to-Standards style communicators?

Identify which items on your "That's for Me!" list will require the Compliant-to-Standards Communication Style.

Watch your favorite TV shows and identify the styles you see. Think about how you would communicate with these people to be effective. Then practice identifying the communication styles you see in meetings and provide what you realize the other person needs, based on the communication style used at that moment.

# CHAPTER 3

# People Reading: Motivators

The second part of people reading is identifying the motivators that are driving a person's actions. Motivators or values are the glue that holds relationships and teams together. When our motivators are aligned, we share a common mission and find fulfilling meaning in our work together.

What really motivates you? As an employee, knowing the answer to this question enables you to identify and raise your hand for projects and assignments that will be meaningful and fulfilling to you.

As a manager or team leader, when you understand how to spot what motivates others, you will be able to offer them assignments, projects, and positions that will align with their motivators. Satisfying work is what makes engagement and collaboration most meaningful. When our motivators are aligned to the work being done, we will be able to build long-term relationships that add deep value over a career.

According to Simon Sinek, author of *Start with Why,* "If you hire people just because they can do a job, they'll work for your money. But if you hire people who believe what you believe, they'll work for you with blood and sweat and tears."

Our beliefs form our values. What we value motivates us into action. According to research done by Eduard Spranger in *Types of Men* (1928) and later G.W. Allport in *The Study of Values* (1960), there are six basic values that show up in the workplace:

**Theoretical:** Wanting to find solutions, using facts and data, and learning and sharing knowledge.

**Utilitarian:** Wanting things to be practical, useful, productive, and financially sound; keeping score perhaps with money or points.

**Individualistic:** Wanting to be part of leadership decision making, striving for a world–class level, and being seen as the best.

**Social:** Wanting to benefit and help others, putting other's needs above one's own, solving people problems.

**Aesthetic:** Wanting things to be artistic, creative, subjective; striving for balance, harmony, and peace.

**Traditional:** Wanting rituals or guidance in how to live or work in the best possible way; having operations or traditions to pass down to others.

A person's top two or three motivators will lock together and be the core reason behind his or her actions. In other words, the top two motivators become the WHY for action. These six motivators are not right or wrong, good or bad. They have no morality. It is how we use them that determines whether they are ethical or not. Each could be used for good or for bad—in ways that lift others up or tear others down. Why we do what we do is tied to our own motivators.

Let's take your knowledge of these six motivators to a deeper level, so you can begin to identify your own drivers. Once you understand your own motivators, then you can think about how to use this knowledge to people read others and discover what inspires them. Knowing how these six motivators work will help you build a lifestyle and career path that will be deeply engaging.

## Theoretical

This motivator has to do with wanting to find solutions, using facts and data, and learning and sharing knowledge.

Do you have a strong desire to learn, grow, and share what you know? If so, Theoretical may be one of your top motivators. Being seen by others as smart or intellectual may also appeal to you.

When this motivator is in your top two, you will find that the following activities or projects are fulfilling:

Systematizing information

Categorizing and analyzing facts and data

Integrating the past and present

Making proposals based on facts and research (not based on emotional arguments)

Understanding theories and asking questions to solve complex problems

Participating in on-going education—multiple certifications and degrees

Supporting educational programs

Reading the latest books or research reports in your field of interest

Using your knowledge to convince others and win arguments with facts

Wanting to know just for the sake of knowing

Asking questions and researching

Participating in book discussion groups

Supporting libraries, bookstores, and research centers in your community

Participating in deep discussions about solving complex social and educational problems

Weeding through lots of information before making decisions

Career paths that reward someone for having the Theoretical motivator include the following:

Education

Statistics

Computer programming

Research

Law

Science

Market research

Medicine

University professor

Anything that requires continuous learning and advanced degrees

When speaking with or selling to people who have High Theoretical motivators, include the following in your presentation:

Give a history of the subject.

Provide facts and research.

Pose problems for them to solve.

Raise questions for exploration and investigation.

Furnish research articles and books on the topic—your resource list.

Give an objective summary of all the options.

Show the deepest level of product knowledge possible; bring the expert if you are not the expert.

Blind spot—the other side of the coin—when people have High Theoretical motivators, they will need to be aware of the following:

Getting too deep in the data and facts and thus turning people off. (People with a High Influence Communication Style can quickly be turned off by this motivator, if they themselves do not have this motivator in their top two.)

Losing sight of practical day-to-day matters from being so intensely focused on learning and solving complex problems. (Forgetting to bathe, pay bills, and feed their pets or children.)

What projects or actions on your own "That's for Me!" list will require you to use, or collaborate with others who use, the Theoretical motivator? Which project will reward the Theoretical motivator?

Do you know anyone who has the Theoretical motivator in his or her top two? Would you enjoy collaborating and networking with that person?

How will you create conversations to engage these people, now that you understand the Theoretical motivator?

## Utilitarian

Wanting things to be practical, useful, productive, and financially sound; keeping score perhaps with money or points.

Do you have a strong desire to be practical, be resourceful, and get a return on your investment of time, energy, and money? Do you have a dashboard of data or goals you track regularly to measure your progress? If so, Utilitarian may be one of your top motivators.

When this motivator is in your top two, you will find that the following activities or projects are fulfilling:

Using a scorecard to track progress and demonstrate momentum towards your goals

Purchasing things that have an investment value

Planning your daily activities to make the most of your time and resources

Providing financial security or being willing to take big risks to become financially free

Being practical in all areas of life

Being future oriented—willing to work hard to achieve results for future gain

Using your resources creatively to solve problems

Working long hours to achieve results

Having an entrepreneurial streak

Seeking career paths that have advancement potential

Organizing systems to create greater efficiencies

Career paths that reward someone for having the Utilitarian motivator include the following:

Entrepreneurship

Owning a business

Sales

Management

Financial advisor

Engineering

Professions that require a focus on practical efficiency and return on investment

Professions with compensation and bonuses directly linked to effort

When speaking with or selling to people who have High Utilitarian motivators, include the following in your presentation:

Show what reality is now; ask them to describe their current reality and what would be most useful to them now.

Explain how they will benefit; what is the return on their investment, if they take the action you are suggesting?

Show why the path you propose is practical and efficient and will create meaningful results.

Demonstrate creativity and futuristic thinking.

Show how they will have control of their time and schedule and can work the hours that are most efficient to get the job done; point out they will be evaluated on the end result.

Blind spot—the other side of the coin—when people have High Utilitarian motivators, they will need to be aware of the following:

Becoming workaholics who do not have breadth to their lives.

Coming across to others who do not have this motivator as being too money-focused or competitive.

Being unwilling to do activities that they consider a waste of time. (They may not see the importance of building a diverse community of people around them for emotional and social support until they are further in their career paths.)

What projects or actions on your own "That's for Me!" list will require you to use, or collaborate with others who use, the Utilitarian motivator? Which project will reward the Utilitarian motivator?

Do you know anyone who has the Utilitarian motivator in his or her top two? Would you enjoy collaborating and networking with that person?

How will you create conversations to engage these people, now that you understand the Utilitarian motivator?

## Social

Wanting to benefit and help others, putting others' needs above your own, solving people problems are important.

Do you have a strong desire to help others and solve complex people issues? If so, Social may be one of your top motivators.

When this motivator is in your top two, you will find that the following activities or projects are fulfilling:

Being generous with time, talents, and resources

Being empathetic to people who are in pain, disadvantaged, hurting

Improving society

Eliminating hate and conflict

Supporting charities and social causes

Promoting fairness to people in all areas of life

Career paths that reward someone for having the Social motivator include the following:

Nursing

Medical support

World relief organizations

Ministry (especially when combined with the Traditional motivator)

Nonprofit charity management

Elementary school teacher

Customer service

Diversity planner

Human resources

Famine relief efforts

Working in a shelter for homeless or abused people, or working in health-care clinics for disadvantaged people (social work)

When speaking with or selling to people who have High Social motivators, include the following in your presentation:

Show how this idea will benefit other people.

Show how this idea will help other people reach their full potential.

Show how this idea will make the community or society better.

Blind spot—the other side of the coin—when people have High Social motivators, they will need to be aware of the following:

Investing time, talents, and resources even when there is no return

Needing to balance planning for their own retirement with giving to others now

Sacrificing bottom-line profit for people-oriented decision making

Avoiding conflict—being blind to issues—if they think confrontation may harm the relationship

Getting upset by people who focus too much on return on investment or have more than their fair share of the world's resources

Staying in a bad relationship or job too long to avoid hurting another person or team by leaving

Giving in or giving too much instead of saying no to people who are asking for help

What projects or actions on your own "That's for Me!" list will require you to use, or collaborate with others who use, the Social motivator?

Do you know anyone who has the Social motivator in his or her top two? Would you enjoy collaborating and networking with that person?

How will you create conversations to engage these people, now that you understand the Social motivator?

## Aesthetic

Wanting things to be artistic, creative, subjective; striving for balance, harmony, and peace.

Do you have a strong desire to be in harmony, creative, in tune with your surroundings, and aware of your inner feelings? If so, Aesthetic may be one of your top motivators.

When this motivator is in your top two, you will find that the following activities or projects are fulfilling:

Doing artistic activities such as painting, music, or gourmet cooking

Preserving natural resources such as forests, parks, and beautiful places

Creating harmony and balance in space, time, and relationships

Finding beauty both in the outside world as well as internally in feelings

Career paths that reward someone for having the Aesthetic motivator include:

Fashion design

Interior design

Architecture

Chef or wine expert

Self-help or therapy

Recycling, restoring, and saving the earth—environmental careers

Theater or drama

Writing

Modeling

Designing jewelry

Feng shui master

Real estate sales and staging

Yoga

Spa services

Graphic design

Or any careers that focus on the following areas:

Creation and appreciation of the finer things in life (ranging from developing luxury brands to being a forester in a national park)

Design, color, music, taste, arrangement, and feelings

Harmony and unity within the physical and internal world

Places that are beautiful or aesthetically pleasing

When speaking with or selling to people who have High Aesthetic motivators, include the following in your presentation:

Acknowledge the importance of their feelings.

Emphasize that there is no right or wrong way; those are subjective.

Use descriptive words, metaphors, and similes.

Speak about harmony, balance, and inner peace.

Ask them to describe the picture as they see it.

Focus on opportunities for self-exploration or improvement.

Ask them to talk about their passion for beauty, form, and harmony.

Blind spot—the other side of the coin—when people have High Aesthetic motivators, they will need to be aware of the following:

Tuning people out, because they are not attuned to the creative and emotional aspects of life.

Losing focus on reality, because they are so deeply engaged in the nuance of color, form, beauty, etc.

Getting stuck in a culture that does not value or reward their motivators and lowers their self-esteem; staying in such a career path because they cannot envision a work place that would appreciate them

What projects or actions on your own "That's for Me!" list will require you to use, or collaborate with others who use, the aesthetic motivator? What projects will reward the Aesthetic motivator?

Do you know anyone who has the Aesthetic motivator in his or her top two? Would you enjoy collaborating and networking with that person?

How will you create conversations to engage these people, now that you understand the Aesthetic motivator?

## Traditional

Wanting rituals or guidance in how to live or work in the best possible way; having operations or traditions to pass down to others.

Do you have a strong desire to follow a system that has a clear purpose or provides a higher meaning in life? Are you looking for the highest meaning in your work or life? Do you follow a religious system faithfully? If so, Traditional may be one of your top motivators.

When this motivator is in your top two, you will find that the following activities or projects are fulfilling:

Having a tradition or system and encouraging others to follow the same system

Creating rules and guidelines that lead to a tradition being passed down and followed faithfully

Supporting organizations and causes that follow the same tradition or system

Rewarding people who place a high value on operating within the tradition

Believing your tradition is the right way to operate and seeking to convert others to this system

Believing strongly in a cause and championing it for others to learn about

Operating with a rulebook or manual for living

Career paths that reward someone for having the Traditional motivator include the following:

Quality control

Religious leadership and teaching

Police officer

Wedding planner

Political campaign manager

When speaking with or selling to people who have High Traditional motivators, include the following in your presentation:

Demonstrate that you understand their beliefs.

Acknowledge their purposes, visions, and missions.

Show how your idea aligns with their traditions and systems.

Do not be thrown off when they only present issues from their own traditions—for them there are no other right paths.

Blind spot—the other side of the coin—when people have High Traditional motivators, they will need to be aware of the following:

Rigidly evaluating other people against their own tradition and standards

Operating according to a closed set of rules and not being open to exploring other possibilities and perspectives

Being idealistic, even when the ideals are unrealistic or impossible

Believing there are absolutes, right and wrong

Dying or killing others for their cause

What projects or actions on your own "That's for Me!" list will require you to use, or collaborate with others who use, the Traditional motivator? Which projects will reward the Traditional motivator?

Do you know anyone who has the Traditional motivator in his or her top two? Would you enjoy collaborating and networking with that person?

How will you create conversations to engage these people, now that you understand the Traditional motivator?

Of the five motivators we have reviewed so far, which are your top two?

I want you to have your answer before you read the last motivator for an important reason, which will become clear as you read about the Individualistic motivator.

Stop now and write out your own list of the five motivators we have discussed in order from highest in importance to lowest. Here they are so you can identify number 1 through 5 based on what is important to you:

_____ Theoretical

_____ Utilitarian

_____ Social

_____ Aesthetic

_____ Traditional

Now that you have these clearly identified for yourself, let's explore the impact of the last one.

## Individualistic

Wanting to be part of leadership decision making, striving for a world-class level, and being seen as the best.

Do you have a strong desire to lead others, make important decisions, and be one of the best? If so, then Individualistic may be one of your top motivators. When this motivator is in the top three, it acts as a booster to the other two near it, causing you to want to take on leadership roles that bring the other two motivators alive in a world-class way. When someone has Individualistic as her top motivator, she is driven to lead and accomplish results—CEO or Managing Director titles will be important to her. When this motivator is number two or three on the list, then that person will be passionate about leading through the other two motivators next to this one.

If this motivator is near the top of your list, you will find that the following activities and projects are fulfilling:

Being in control of the project and team

Directing the destiny of others and organizations

Being recognized for the achievements of an organization, industry, or department

Being willing to work long and hard to achieve the highest-level position

Feeling like life and work is a chess game; looking for ways to strategically move in relationships and alliances that further your causes and beliefs

Career paths that reward someone for having the Individualistic motivator include the following:

Roles with access to advancement, limelight, leadership, strategic relationships, and key alliances

Chief executive officer

Business owner

Industry or trade association president

Politician

Professional athlete

When this motivator is in your top three, it will be played out through leadership roles that bring alive your other top motivators. Here are some clues to help you see when someone has this motivator along with the others:

**Individualistic and Theoretical:** Will have a drive to be known as an expert or guru in a particular field, a college professor of an Ivy League university, or business leader like chief scientific officer of a world-class organization. Examples: Albert Einstein, Mark Zuckerberg, Alan Greenspan.

**Individualistic and Utilitarian:** Will want to gain wealth and maximize resources in leadership. Examples: Donald Trump, Henry Ford, Warren Buffett, Ben Franklin.

**Individualistic and Aesthetic:** Will want to use creative abilities to achieve form, harmony, and beauty—create the ideal version of what they are focused on. Examples: Ralph Lauren, Mary Kay Ash, Rachael Ray, Tyra Banks, Heidi Klum.

**Individualistic and Social:** Will want to lead humanitarian causes to make the world a better place for others. Examples: Rachel Carson, Brad Pitt and Angelina Jolie, Florence Nightingale, Mother Teresa.

**Individualistic and Traditional:** Will want to guide people in using a particular system for operating or living. Examples: Pope John Paul II, Martin Luther, and Billy Graham in Christianity; Dr. Edwards Deming in Quality Management practices.

When speaking with or selling to people who have High Individualistic motivators, include the following in your presentation:

Provide the big picture and how the puzzle pieces interlock with your ideas.

Explain how your idea enables advancement, growth, and leadership.

Create opportunities for achieving world-class distinctions and benchmarks.

Provide the freedom to make decisions and take risks.

Create plans for providing a mastermind team that ensures all bases are covered and will lead to best-in-class thinking.

Blind spot—the other side of the coin—when people have High Individualistic motivators, they will need to be aware of the following:

Being too overpowering, squashing other people's ideas and creativity

Bullying others, by using their titles or power to push ideas ahead when they are not the best ideas available

Having a low tolerance for people who do not challenge themselves

## Your Motivators and Your Organization's Motivators— Do You Have Alignment?

Why does your organization exist? How would you identify the hierarchy of motivators in your organization?

Dave and Wendy Ulrich collaborated to write *The Why of Work: How Great Leaders Build Abundant Organizations That Win*. They explain how leaders can influence whether workers perceive their work as meaningful. Their recommendations, based on extensive research and experience in organizations and psychology, provide a guide for creating meaning with tangible value to employees, customers, investors, and communities. They make the case that part of leadership includes helping employees build professional connections and friendships because building personal strengths expands organizational capabilities, increases performance, and improves results.

The Ulrichs describe human beings as "meaning-making machines" who seek and often find inherent value in making sense of life. Dave and Wendy Ulrich ask these seven questions:

1. What am I known for?
2. Where am I going?
3. Whom do I travel with?
4. How do I build a positive work environment?
5. What challenges interest me?
6. How do I respond to disposability and change?
7. What delights me?

These questions are much easier to answer when we understand our own workplace motivators. Answer these questions for yourself, and then see if you can answer them for your organization. The answers will provide clarity about your organization's motivators. Do you align well, based on your motivators?

Early in my career, I had the opportunity to work with several great leaders, people who engaged me deeply in conversations about why we were doing what we were doing and how my own goals fit into the work we were doing. It was fun to go to work and be part of that high-performing team. About fifteen years into my professional career, I was moved to a new organization and reported to the CEO. Within six months, I realized my new boss, the most senior leader of the organization, did not know how to play to the strengths of his team members. He did not know how to identify or develop star performers to grow the business. I realized that this blind spot in his capabilities (and his unwillingness to face it) was costing the organization a great deal, and it was stifling the potential of the team. When I had that realization, I made the decision to focus my own career on developing high performers who aspire to be leaders. I wanted to ensure that future leaders had the right combination of abilities to succeed, not just for themselves, but also for the teams of people they would be guiding. If my boss had learned the abilities I am sharing with you in this book, I would likely still be working for that corporation! But when I realized that we did not share the same values, I knew that, for me to fully live my values, I needed to leave. So I designed a role for myself around my values and beliefs. What I do everyday is based on my values. I'm living my "That's for Me!" list. Are you ready to do the same?

In *Start With Why,* Simon Sinek says: "Our need to belong is not rational, but it is a constant that exists across all people in all cultures. It is a feeling we get when those around us share our values and beliefs. When we feel like we belong, we feel connected and we feel safe. As humans we crave the feeling and we seek it out . . . The goal of business should not be to do business with anyone who simply wants what you have. It should be to focus on the people who believe what you believe. When we are selective about doing business with those who believe in our WHY, trust emerges."

Why do you work where you do? The answer to that question reflects your values and your emotional set point.

We all want to add substantial value in our lives through our relationships and our work. Meaning or the absence of meaning is determined by our ability to live our values and to bring our workplace motivators alive in our organizations. When we are living an adventurer story, we work because we are searching for meaning; we want to be inspired and to inspire others. When we are living our values, how to do that becomes clearer. When we collaborate in our work with a team, our shared purpose gives meaning and direction, so that each team member has the potential to add substantial value. This makes work meaningful.

Such meaning also has market value because, as the Ulrichs' research suggests, "meaningful work solves real problems, contributes real benefits, and thus adds real value to customers and investors." In this context, the Ulrichs introduce the idea of the "abundant organization." They identify an abundant organization's dominant characteristics as, "a work setting in which individuals coordinate their aspirations and actions to create meaning for themselves, value for stakeholders, and hope for humanity at large" and "[have] enough of the things that matter most: creativity, hope, resilience, determination, resourcefulness, and leadership; a profitable enterprise that concentrates on opportunities, potentialities, synergies, and fulfillment of a diversity of human needs and experiences; and especially when times are tough, a social as well as economic force that can bring order, integrity, and purpose out of chaos and disintegration." An abundant organization gives meaning to everyone involved, by offering a community and a physical environment within which to thrive as human beings; their contributions, in turn, create a decisive competitive advantage for the organization while increasing and enhancing its market as well as its social value.

The underlying cause of most problems in the workplace is a deficit of both meaning and purpose—a lack of clear motivators and alignment with a group of people who want to collaborate to create value. To become and then remain abundant, the leaders in an organization need to guide people, to leverage their strengths, and to serve their core values, doing so with their career objectives in alignment to their organization's strategic objectives.

Just as we describe people reading a person, you can use your understanding of communication styles and motivators to look at the predominant patterns in an organization or a team.

## People Reading: Motivators Application Exercise

Identify what you think your peers', team members', and boss's top motivators are.

Practice creating conversations and giving assignments that play to and draw on each type of motivator. For example, if you are speaking with a team member about an assignment and you know that person's top two motivators are Theoretical and Utilitarian, what words would you use? What language would be important for you to use to keep your team member engaged?

In this case, you would want to point out the opportunities for practical learning, draw out the importance of doing research, ask questions about how progress could be measured, and invite suggestions for how things could be improved.

Review your "That's for Me!" list. Look at each item on your list and ask yourself why you want to do it. Asking yourself why you want to create something forces you to examine, "What is my motivation? What am I passionate about?" If you have not done enough exploring to know the answer to this question, then take the time to carefully examine your motivation. Be diligent about discovering your core passions. What is the emotional connection you have with your goals? Motivation requires emotion; we want to be passionate about what we are creating in order to inspire others to join us. What projects or actions on your own "That's for Me!" list will require you to use, or collaborate with each type of motivator? For example, which projects will reward the Individualist motivator? Which ones will reward the Social motivator?

Consider whom you know that exhibits each motivator? Would you enjoy collaborating with these people based on motivators? Why or why not?

How will you create conversations to engage these people now that you understand each motivator?

# CHAPTER 4

# People Reading: Emotional Intelligence

Do you like puppies? Imagine that you are in your office and someone brings in two cute little puppies. What are you likely to feel? For some people, the puppies will trigger playful and happy feelings. But for others, the interruption will trigger feelings of annoyance; they might think, "Why is someone bringing puppies into the workplace when we have so much work to do?"

Now imagine Juan turns up the song he is listening to so it is very loud. He is in the office, seemingly oblivious to the people who are now starting to look at him. What are you likely to feel? Again, the people observing Juan will have different reactions. Some will stop what they are doing and join in the spontaneous music dance break; others will roll their eyes, clearly annoyed at his inconsiderate behavior. There is not one emotions map that fits all of us. Emotionally intelligent people understand their own emotions map and then begin to see the common patterns in the way people display their emotions.

Our feelings are triggered by our thoughts and by what is happening around us. What triggers joy in you may not trigger joy in me and vice versa, because the wiring of our brains is different.

The third part of people reading involves being able to identify what you are feeling and then what another person is likely feeling in the moment. You want to consider how those emotions will affect what you are doing together now. Knowing how your own emotion is affecting your actions and how another person's current emotion is affecting his or her thinking and actions is vital to people reading and effective collaboration. To be able to do this in a conversation requires developing emotional intelligence first.

Emotional intelligence includes five abilities: self-awareness, self-regulation, motivation, empathy, and social skills. Let's discuss each of these abilities so that you can identify which ones may need more developing in order for you to get better results when people reading and collaborating with others.

## Self-Awareness

The ability to identify what we ourselves are feeling in the moment is self-awareness. It is useful to know there are seven core emotions. All the other words we use to describe emotions are symptoms of these seven states. Each of these states is identified by a different chemical combination that comes from our amygdala, inside our brains. We are always marinating in one of these chemical combinations:

**Love:** passion for what we are doing or whom we are with

**Joy:** excitement, jubilation, happiness

**Hope:** willingness to see new possibilities

**Envy:** jealousy, wishing we had something someone else has

**Sadness:** despair, longing for yesterday or experiencing loss

**Anger:** frustration, rage, something or someone has crossed our boundaries

**Fear:** the need to be safe or anxiety about the unknown

These emotions are listed from the highest, lightest feeling (love) to the lowest, heaviest feeling (fear). You may use other words to represent the scale for yourself; it is your ability to identify the range and the corresponding thinking for yourself that is most important and how you want to use the emotion to move forward that is most powerful.

Have you ever almost been in a car accident? What happened a few seconds after you recognized you were not in an accident? Did you have what I call "jelly legs," where your whole body shakes? Chemicals triggering fear just rushed through your whole body. The amygdala in the brain sends these chemicals through your body when you have this shift in your emotional state. Whether you are aware of it or not, you are always marinating in an emotion. Once an emotional state has been triggered, the effects last at least four hours, unless you know how to shift yourself. If you feel a rush of anger, the chemicals that correspond to anger will be in your body for four hours until they dissipate or you intentionally refocus yourself. However, if you keep retelling yourself the story of why you are angry, you could stay in that marinade for many hours or days. The story plot line you create keeps triggering emotion. Use your feelings to inform your next actions. You can think your way into another emotional state if you understand how to self-regulate.

> *When I'm upset with a situation or a person, I've learned not to hit the send button on an e-mail. I'll come back and re-read it the next day, when the anger has dissipated. Just because I feel angry does not mean the person I am communicating with needs to know that is what I am feeling. Better to request what I want going forward than to get mired down in anger that is unproductive."*
> —Alan Sterner, Owner and Director of Purpose and Passion, Sterner Insurance Agency

Imagine you are standing at an elevator. You get onto the elevator and press a button—floor 2. As the door opens, you look out and see angry people everywhere. This whole floor is filled with anger vibes and experiences. You decide not to get out on that floor. You press the button for floor 5. As the elevator doors open, you realize this is a very different place. Everyone looks hopeful; there are lots of possibilities, and optimism flows on this floor. When you become highly aware of your ability to choose what you are feeling you will be able to move up the emotional scale, because you know what triggers you to feel love, joy, and hope. You can also begin to choose how you want to guide yourself through times when you feel fear, anger, or sadness. When you have a high level of self-awareness, you can also choose activities, projects, assignments, and people who trigger you into higher levels of feeling. As your self-awareness grows, you develop confidence that you know how to deal with any emotion you experience. But as with any skill, developing this takes practice.

Do you want to work with someone who is afraid and angry much of the time or with someone who is excited and hopeful much of the time? I've asked thousands of people this question, and so far no one has told me he or she prefers to work in an office with colleagues who are fearful and angry. Fear and anger serve a meaningful purpose if you use them wisely and do not get stuck in them as a way of being. If you learn to channel fear, anger, or sadness correctly, you do not have to stay stuck in them. You can begin to deliberately move your normal emotional set point up the scale. (An emotional set point is the emotion you habitually dwell in—a kind of emotional thermostat setting. My thermostat happens to be set at 74 degrees at the moment. Sometimes the temperature in the room is higher or lower, but most of the time it hovers around the set point of 74 degrees. Similarly, a happy person might have an emotional set point in the joy range, where a Debbie Downer remains fixed in the sadness or fear range.)

Each emotion serves a purpose for us and our ability to collaborate with others. Let's look at each emotion through the lens of collaboration:

## Love

When you feel passionate about a project, an experience, or working with a person or a team, you are going to be inspired. You will also likely be inspiring to others. High energy, focused attention, and clear thinking show up in you. When you find yourself loving what you do, milk the experience for more! Notice what triggered this emotional response and how it affects your body, creating more opportunities to soak in the marinade of pleasure-inducing chemicals. Your being in this state will be uplifting to others around you. You will express gratitude and appreciation when you are in this state. You will also be able to create solutions and new ideas from this state. Choose this state as often as possible by putting yourself in places and relationships that cause you to feel love.

## Joy

When you feel excited, happy, jubilant, and grateful, it shows in the way you think more creatively and listen more readily to new ideas and suggestions from others. You may feel like you are walking on sunshine, ready for an adventure. Joy feels good—emotionally and physically—so you want to notice what triggers this emotion so you can create more experiences that bring you to this happy state. Others will see in your expressions and choice of words that you are in a good emotional place—you look happy. You will also be able to create solutions and new ideas in this state. Take actions and connect with people who often cause you to feel joy.

## Hope

When you see new pathways, and you believe that a solution is possible, you discover energy you didn't know you had. Trying something new opens you to still more possibilities, which in turn replenishes your sense of hope and your well of energy. Notice when hope shows up in your thinking, and tune into how it affects your body. Ask yourself, "What thinking and actions do I want to engage in to bring the feeling of hope alive?"

### Envy

When someone else has an experience or a thing you want, it can cause the emotional marinade of envy or jealousy. Catch this state early and ask yourself, "What is it that I see that I want to create for myself?" Add that experience or thing to your "That's for Me!" list. Remind yourself that you have learned how to do many things, and you can now learn how to do or set up the experience that you want for yourself. Begin to see envy as an emotion that helps you inspire yourself to create more and to grow. If you listen to what is happening in your thoughts and redirect your thinking, the green-eyed, resentful monster does not have to emerge from the chemical rush of envy through your body. Is there someone or some situation you feel jealous of? Can you use that emotion to create something more or better for yourself and others? Describe what you want to create for yourself, add it to your "That's for Me!" list, and move forward whenever you feel envy.

### Sadness

When you experience loss or when you do not reach a goal, it is normal to feel let down. Sadness is an emotion that asks you to learn from the experience you have had. When you catch yourself feeling sad, ask yourself, "What did I or could I learn from this experience? How could I share what I have learned in a way that would be helpful to me and others?" You may have to ask these questions over several days or months to process yourself through the feeling. Writing in a journal to uncover your own learning is the first step. Many people ignore the sadness, and then it becomes deeper because, if you ignore your own feelings, you cannot grow. Instead, this creates a stuck experience. Being depressed is a signal that you have not been listening to or respectful of your own voice; there is a habituated sadness set point. A habituated emotional set point is what happens when you feel one emotion over a long period of time—you learn to relate to that chemical marinade as if it were normal. Perhaps you feel shut down. When you catch yourself in sadness, ask yourself, "What are the lessons and the learning from this experience?" After you are clear on what you learned, share it with at least one other person to be helpful. Serve others with your learning. When you do this, you will begin to experience a shift in your feelings and you can move up the emotions scale.

It is not uncommon for someone moving up from sadness to feel jealous of others who did not go through this sad experience. Keep moving through that, stay focused on creating something better, something uplifting, and you will move up to hope and joy. If you notice that someone else seems to be feeling sad, you might ask, "What is happening for you? What have you learned from this experience? How could your experience be helpful to others?" By being there for another person and deeply listening and then asking questions that enable him or her to focus up the emotion scale, you can help guide others through stuck spots too.

> A Buddhist student asked his teacher during a meditation retreat, "I am very discouraged. What should I do?" The teacher replied, "Encourage others."

## Anger

When your boundaries have been crossed, you feel anger, so that you have the energy and the focus to stand up for yourself. When your boundaries have been crossed, identify what the real issue is for you. What is it you really want? Then think through how to ask for what you want in a way that the person who has the power to give it to you can hear. Use his communication style, and think the issue through from his perspective. Instead of behaving from frustration and coming across as angry, it may be better to make a clear request first. Often the person who has crossed your boundaries does not know that he has done so. It may be perfectly obvious to you, but not to him. Make your request from the place of assuming good intentions. This approach will frequently do the trick and clean up the issue. When people ignore their own anger, they begin to show up as bitter and resentful. If your request for your boundaries to be honored is ignored, then you will feel angry for being ignored and disrespected. That requires a conversation for breakdown and conflict resolution (these conversations are discussed in the chapter on conflict resolution and the Appendix). If not resolved well, it may cause you to find new people to work with, who honor your boundaries and treat you with respect. Anger that is not dealt with will lead to fear and shutdown.

### Fear

Fear has two faces. When you are driving 80 miles per hour in a 30-mile-per-hour zone, you want to feel fear to trigger a reaction to slow down. If you are doing jumping jacks on the edge of a cliff, you want to feel fear so that you stop and move back to where it is safe. Fear is useful when it reins you in, if you need to be reined in.

The other face of fear may be seen when you do not know how to do something that you need to do in order to move forward. You hold yourself back or limit yourself with small thinking and stuck behavior patterns. Perhaps you are asked to deliver a speech to 200 people and you have never spoken to a large group before. Do you freeze and let your limited beliefs stop you, or do you say, "I'm going to learn how." What are you likely to feel if you are asked to speak to a large audience about something you have deep expertise in? Many people experience fear and limit themselves, even though speaking to groups is a learnable skill. When you rein yourself in and hold on tight, you are acting out of fear. Victim story patterns are born out of fear-based thinking. This is a sign that you need to re-wire your thinking, to instead say something like this: "I have learned how to do many complex things. I can talk, walk, write, drive, sing, dance, play tennis, and make lasagna! I was not born knowing how to do any of these things. All of these required me to learn. I can learn! If someone else learned how to do this, then I am likely to be able to learn how to do it too. Do I want to teach myself or find a coach who will use my learning style to teach me? How can I break it down step-by-step? I can learn how to do this!"

This kind of self-talk can get us out of fear. Begin to catch yourself when you are afraid and then ask yourself, "Which type of fear is this? How do I want to use this feeling to guide my next actions?" Then process yourself through the emotion and move yourself up the emotional scale so that you do not stay stuck in fear. Remember, not everything you think is the truth; challenge, change, or channel your thinking to create new possibilities for yourself.

Many people have a fear of meeting new people or of trying to make new friends. They tell themselves that they were not good at relationships in the past. The real truth is they did not know how. Or perhaps when they were young, they had bad experiences with others who had very different communication styles and motivators, and they are still stuck in that experience. People reading is the new skill to learn in these situations. Your ability to people read enables you to build new relationships that are meaningful.

Which emotion are you feeling now? In what ways is that emotion affecting how you are holding your body? What is happening in your body? How is that emotion affecting the thoughts you are experiencing and the possibilities you see at this moment? To raise your own self-awareness, begin to randomly track which emotion you are feeling at various times during the day. Also ask yourself, "What triggered that emotion?" Listen to your self-talk to catch this in the moment. For example, if you notice yourself feeling joyful, you may experience that your body feels light and your posture is great. The predominant thought spinning through your mind is how much you are enjoying your current project. Perhaps hours later you notice yourself feeling sad, and your posture is slumped over, and you keep having the same thought that you do not have enough friends. Ask yourself, "How do I want to use this emotion to inform my next actions?"

### What Patterns Do You Notice?

By doing this over time, you will be able to identify your emotional set point or the range of emotions you tend to experience. Some people vacillate between joy and hope much of the time. Others move from anger to fear much of the time. The only way to identify these tendencies is to randomly track the emotion you are feeling in the moment over a period of a month or two. The goal is to move yourself up the emotional scale, so that most of the time you are coming from the highest emotions you have access to.

### What Do You Notice? What Is Your Emotional Set Point?

Every emotion serves a purpose. When you learn to use this internal guidance system well, you can be proactive instead of reactive, which will ultimately lead to making better decisions. Most people that I coach have not learned how to use their emotional guidance system wisely. I was emotionally illiterate until I learned how to identify what I was feeling and then consciously use that awareness to direct my next actions. Of course, this took practice. I worked with a coach who challenged me to grow in new ways as I developed my emotional intelligence. Lots of practice!

After you develop self-awareness, then focus on self-regulation. Self-regulation is the ability to use an emotion wisely. You may need to regulate yourself in all of the seven emotions to begin to use them in a way that will generate collaboration and lead to the desired results.

## Self-Regulation

Emotional hijacks or impulsive behavior result when we do not have strong muscles in self-regulation. If we do not have strong self-regulation muscles, we can be overcome by any of the emotions and either take actions that we will regret later or not take actions needed to achieve the results we desire.

We need the self-regulation ability so that we can intentionally process ourselves through emotions or guide ourselves to use our emotions in a healthy way. When we have strong self-regulation ability, we can guide ourselves, and then others, through emotional stuck spots. We no longer act in unintended ways that cause more problems, such as kicking the dog or picking fights about the wrong stuff. I call this "coming out sideways." Stop coming out sideways with others and acknowledge the real feelings you are experiencing.

Here are some examples of self-regulation in action: If I catch myself feeling anger, I now know to ask, "What or who crossed my boundaries? Whom do I need to speak with to clean up the boundary violation?" When we do this, anger becomes a signal that we can catch early on. We do not have to live in resentment or bitterness if we catch the feeling of anger early on and take the actions we need to take. This will require people reading—identifying another person's communication style and motivators and asking for what we want, so that he or she can understand why the issue is important to us. Identifying our anger and the violations that trigger it enables us to create a better career path or life for ourselves and others.

Self-regulation of fear can be complex, because in some cases we need to honor fear and in others we need to overcome it. Fear can be a signal to stop what we are doing, as in the example of driving 80 miles per hour in a 30-mile-per-hour zone. We want to feel fear so that we will slow down. But fear can also be an obstacle to reaching our full potential, as in the example of public speaking mentioned before. When we stop ourselves from learning what we need to know in order to create new results in our lives, fear becomes a problem. That is when we need to move forward, despite the fear.

There are times when I am confronted with a situation that calls for skills or abilities I do not currently have, and I will feel fear. When that happens, I need to look the fear in the eye and recognize what it is that I need to learn how to do. As an executive coach, I often work with clients who have identified fears in their professional lives: some feel fear when they are promoted to a higher level of leadership, or need to build new relationships with people they do not know or when they need to attend association meetings to learn about their industry and they do not know anyone there, or when they are expected to deliver a presentation to a large audience. The fear that comes with learning new skills can stifle our ability to learn. We have to self-regulate and keep ourselves moving forward to remain focused on the prize at the end of the learning—mastery of a new ability. When we feel paralyzed by fear, we must remind ourselves of what we have learned in the past and reassure ourselves that we are able to learn new skills now.

Jealousy or envy is an emotion that can inspire us to ask ourselves, "What is it that the other person has or experiences that I also want to have or experience for myself?" You can do, have, or experience this in your own way too! Use it as inspiration. The moment I catch myself in a state of envy, I immediately guide the emotion into hope by clarifying for myself what I now realize I want to add to my "That's for Me!" list. I remind myself that I've been able to create many breakthrough results in my career and life by being aware of this. If I can do it, you can do it too! Do you see in this example that self-awareness comes before self-regulation?

Sadness is a signal that we have not yet learned a lesson that our experience wants us to integrate into our lives. It is common to feel sad when you lose something valued, such as a job, relationship, dream, or person who was meaningful. When you catch yourself feeling sad, ask, "What can I learn from this situation? What is the message of the experience for me? How long would the person I am missing want me to be sad?" Write your answers each time you notice yourself feeling sadness. Then begin to explore ways you can share your learning with others, so that they do not have to experience the loss you experienced. Make a difference with your learning. Soon you will find the sadness lifts, and you are able to move onto a higher level of feeling. If we do not do this, sadness can become a black hole that leads to depression.

When you have healthy self-regulation muscles, you will be able to observe your own awareness and recognize when to rein yourself in or pick up your pace in your behavior. Self-regulation shows up in how we manage these elements of daily life:

**Time:** We prioritize what will bring us love, joy, passion, hope.

**Space:** We create organized spaces that enable us to accomplish what we want.

**Health:** We eat nutrient-dense foods and exercise so our bodies feel good and remain healthy.

**Network of colleagues and friends:** We have relationships that are meaningful, and we build a community of people we enjoy connecting with.

**Money:** We use our resources wisely and plan our spending to meet our needs before our wants, and we save to create the future we desire.

## Motivation

In the previous chapter, we talked a great deal about being able to identify what motivates you. When you understand your own motivators, you can raise your hand for activities, projects, positions, and relationships that will align with them. As a result, you will feel inspired, motivated, and engaged in your work. You will be able to identify others that are motivated and engaged in their work also. You can ask other people questions about which of the motivators are most inspiring to them. With this information, you will be able to give assignments that trigger emotional connection for the people you collaborate with.

I believe the purpose of life is to experience love and joy. Do you agree? We want to live our lives from the top of the emotional scale as much as we can. The important thing to know about emotional intelligence is that when we value our own emotional well-being, we will put ourselves in assignments and roles that play to our top motivators. We will value feeling love, passion, and joy. We will not be willing to stay in relationships or roles that frequently trigger in us feelings of fear, anger or sadness. If we are spending most of our time marinating in fear, anger, or sadness, then it is time to make some shifts in our thinking and behavior to improve our motivation level.

## Empathy

In a conversation or meeting, do you identify what the other person is likely feeling now? How do you use this awareness to build conversations with others?

Empathy occurs when we confirm or clarify what we think the other person may be feeling, given the current circumstances. When we respect and honor another person's feelings, we are seen as having empathy. When we ignore or judge others or tell them they should not feel what they are feeling, then we are not being empathetic.

Our ability to guide others to use their emotions in healthy ways depends on our ability to create empathetic rapport. People who have this ability are known as great listeners and inspirers. We feel like kindred spirits with people who have these abilities.

Have you ever stood at the back of a boat and watched the wake created as the boat moves through the water? We create a similar emotional wake as we move through our conversations with others. Do you observe the emotional wake in the relationships around you? Do you know someone who seems angry much of the time? Or maybe you know someone who seems sad? Does another person come to mind who seems happy, joyful, or optimistic most of the time? What do you notice about the emotional wake that ripples from these people? You also are known for an emotional wake. Do you know what it is?

Have you ever seen the Debbie Downer skits on *Saturday Night Live*? If not, check them out on YouTube. They provide a great example of emotional wake.

When you are talking with someone who seems angry, you can calmly ask her to help you understand what has triggered the anger. When you see someone who appears jealous, you can help him to articulate what he's seen that he wants. Then encourage him to create a goal to move toward it. "What would need to exist for you to have or experience that too?" you may ask. When you see someone who seems to be afraid, you may ask that person if there is something she needs to slow down or be brave and face head on, or if there is something she does not know how to do in order to accomplish what she wants. Your ability to guide others through their emotional stuck spots will make you a trusted advisor.

Your emotional set point is like a wave or wake that affects how people see, hear, and experience you. If you want to be known as a leader who inspires other people in a positive way, you will need to be able to deliberately use the full range of emotions yourself.

## Social Skills

Social skills can be defined as our ability to engage a person, a team, or a group of individuals and keep them moving forward toward common goals. We have to develop the previously discussed abilities in order to have good social skills. People reading, listening, and collaborating are the ingredients of strong social skills.

*"As leaders, we are in the emotional transportation business."*
—Peter Guber

## People Reading: Emotional Intelligence Application Exercise

What triggers or causes you to feel each of the following states?

Love

Joy

Hope

Envy

Sadness

Anger

Fear

Identify three predictable ways you could trigger each of these emotions in yourself. Write your answers in a learning journal now. What stories do you tell that generate each emotional state?

### Action to Take for Each Emotion

When you feel love, joy, and hope, notice what triggered this state and marinate in it longer.

When you feel envy, ask yourself: "What could I add to my 'That's for Me!' list? What goals could this inspire me to set for myself? What actions could I take to move in a direction that would inspire me more, so that I am not jealous of someone else but instead I am focused on what I want to create next?"

When you feel sad, ask yourself: "What have I lost? (It may be a person, an experience, or a dream that you realize will not happen.) What have I learned from this experience that I can apply to my future? Is there someone else that I can share this

learning with in a meaningful way that would make the experience of beneficial?"

When you feel anger, ask yourself: "What crossed my
boundaries? What is my request? Whom do I need to speak
with to clean up the boundary violation?"

When you feel fear, ask yourself: "Which type of fear is
this—the kind that indicates I need to pull myself back or the
kind that points out it is time to be brave and learn how to do
something I do not yet know how to do? If it is a signal to slow
down or stop something, what action do I want to take next? If
it is a signal that I do not yet know how to do something that I
want to learn how to do, who could guide me? Who knows
how to do this as a star performer that I could learn from?"

For the next 30 days, three times each day, randomly ask
yourself the question, "What am I feeling now?" Let your
answer inform your next actions. Notice how your emotions
are an internal guidance system that can help you to be more
effective when you use them wisely. Value each emotion, recognizing that all emotions serve a productive purpose if we will
use them to inform our actions and not let them hijack us into
action.

Review your "That's for Me!" list and notice what you feel.

When you read the "I Did It!" section at the end of your list,
what do you feel?

# Tying Together People Reading

When you are able to identify a person's or group's motivators, preferred communication style, and which emotion they are currently marinating in, you are able to create more effective conversations and relationships. Recently a coaching client of mine who spent six months focused on mastering people-reading skills shared this with me in our final wrap-up session: "Knowing how to people read in the moment is the most profound skill I've ever learned. I was judgmental of peers and bosses, and I did not realize what it was costing me in my professional growth. As a result, I am now more aware and more intentional about the conversations I create. I adapt easily when I need to. I also have realized when I need to change other people's perspectives of me and my team, and I know how to do that now." Our ability to people read is most important in relationships that are new, challenging, or changing. Let's bring these pieces together with several stories that highlight the importance of being able to use these skills as a peer, a manager, and a team.

## Anya's Story

Anya called me crying. She was shocked. Anya was in fear. I already knew from previous conversations that Anya's preferred communication style is High Steady and her highest two motivators are Social and Theoretical. Her lowest motivator is Individualistic.

Anya was almost hysterical on the phone. I asked her to take a few deep breaths, and then I said, "Anya, keep breathing deeply as you slowly share with me what happened." Anya's new manager, Meeta, had given her a "not meeting expectations" rating on her annual review and said she expected Anya to be put on a Performance Improvement Plan. Meeta also said that Anya would need to attend training to learn to be more effective in her role.

Anya's new manager had arrived in September, when her former manager left the company. Now, six months later, the new manager, Meeta, who seems to prefer the Dominant Communication Style, was giving Anya a "not meeting expectations rating" in several of her key accountabilities from the previous year. Anya began to spiral down emotionally as soon as she saw the performance review document that was e-mailed to her by her new manager. She could not think clearly. Anya was in the grip of an emotional hijacking that triggered deep fear. An emotional hijacking is what happens when an emotion takes over and we lose our ability to think clearly.

According to Anya, when she met with the new manager to discuss her review, it did not seem like her manager was willing to listen. I asked Anya several more questions and learned that Anya had completed the assignments now being given a "not meeting expectations rating" before her new manager's arrival. Her former manager had even congratulated Anya on an outstanding job and sent her an e-mail saying so. Apparently, that feedback had not been shared with Meeta, her new manager. Or if it had, Meeta had misplaced it. Clearly, Anya had the responsibility to show Meeta the completed work and the previous manager's communication about the results, but she had not done this, because she was so offended by Meeta's direct, confident communication.

I realized that Anya was afraid and needed to think the situation through from another emotion in order to see a solution. I suggested Anya ask for another meeting to discuss the review, so that it was not left as things were now. If she did not address this situation with Meeta, Anya would become very resentful and bitter. When Anya did make the request to meet on this matter, Meeta invited the human resources manager to attend the meeting too and sent an outlook e-mail inviting them to meet in two days.

Meeta's response caused Anya to feel more anxious. Anya told me she wondered whether they were going to fire her at the meeting. Again, these were signs that Anya was spiraling in fear and not speaking from her abilities. High Steady style communicators often need encouragement to stand up for themselves, to be confident and directly ask for what they want.

Anya had to create a new conversation to ask for what she wanted and demonstrate that her work did meet expectations earlier in the year. During the next meeting, Anya had the e-mails from her previous boss saying that the expectations had been exceeded. I coached Anya to begin this conversation by saying: "You've offered developmental training, and I am very interested in that possibility. And I would like to direct your attention to these e-mails from my previous boss. I am requesting that the rating be changed on my current review due to these facts. I did complete the tasks that were rated as incomplete; here is the proof from e-mails that my previous manager sent me. If you believe I need development training, I am willing to take the actions you recommend to develop my abilities." Much to Anya's surprise, the new manager and HR manager agreed to change the review in light of these facts.

After the meeting, I advised Anya to send a handwritten thank-you note to each manager, thanking them both for taking the time to listen to her point of view, for changing her review, and for building trust in their relationship.

Anya had to process through her fear in order to create new outcomes in these important game-changing conversations. Despite her preferred High Steady style, Anya needed to speak confidently and directly in order to be heard by a manager with a High Dominant Communication Style. This interaction helped Anya to build her confidence in asking for what she wanted from her new boss. For Anya, this experience of moving through the fear and getting new results dramatically changed how she felt about her work and her new boss.

## Jacqueline and Ben's Story

Jacqueline is naturally fast-paced and intense, a real go-getter. She is focused on practical results that help grow the global business she has been in for several years. She is motivated to achieve growth, to be practical, and to lead a world-class organization. Jacqueline wants to be seen as a strategic leader and part of the best team.

Ben is the owner of the global engineering consulting firm where Jacqueline works. He started this company on his own 20 years ago and has watched it grow every year to be a billion-dollar organization now. Ben values research, data, logic, and problem-solving ability. He even teaches a course on logic and problem solving at his MBA alma mater once a year and invites his new employees to sit in, because these topics are so important to him. He also likes to implement large-scale projects with little visibility for him personally. He and his teams have achieved major wins and have been featured in industry magazines, because of the amazing results of his firm.

Ben's story about Jacqueline is that she is "too arrogant and defensive." He developed this view after he received feedback from her employees over a year ago that she was difficult to report to because she was pushy, bossy, and domineering. She did not listen to or engage others; she just plowed ahead with her own agenda.

Ben has not reached out to connect with Jacqueline much in the past year; he had turned her over to an executive coach and disappeared to work on other parts of the business. She thinks Ben is aloof with her now. Because they have had little interaction this year, Ben has not seen the significant growth Jacqueline has experienced.

Jacqueline admits that she did behave exclusively in a High Dominant style before working with a coach and learning how to people read. Since then she has changed her communication interaction with her employees and peers. Now she is able to identify the communication needs and the motivators of the meeting or project she is working on and adapt to what is needed to create momentum. She also knows when and how to bring the right people into a project to gain different perspectives. She values different styles of communicating and motivators that may show her how to get the desired results. A year ago, this would not have crossed Jacqueline's mind. She would have expected everyone to adapt to her style.

Although Ben encouraged Jacqueline to work with an executive coach, he has not spent time with her to see the changes in her behavior. Jacqueline now wants him to recognize her development, so that she will have opportunities to grow in her career with his company. Jacqueline believes that in the next six months there will be an opportunity to lead a new division, and she wants to be considered for that role. For this to happen, Ben will need to see her growth. How can Jacqueline collaborate with Ben so he can see that she has changed the way she interacts with her staff and peers?

What would you ask or suggest if you were guiding Jacqueline? Think through the dynamics, based on what you understand about this situation.

What is Jacqueline's preferred communication style? What are her motivators?

What is Ben's preferred communication style likely to be? What are his motivators? What might you conclude about his maturity level?

What Jacqueline and I decided to do: Ben is someone who wants the data, facts, and research. His style is very different from Jacqueline's, so she has to take that into account in how she presents him with her development. Because Jacqueline had grown so much in the year and we wanted others to reflect on her recent growth, we completed a 360 survey, knowing the results would also yield a report that could be shown to Ben.

I do these 360 surveys in two ways. First, I invite people to go on-line and complete a survey about the leadership style or the emotional intelligence of the person I am working with. Up to 100 people can respond. Since Jacqueline has a large staff, I decided to use this type of survey for them. When I had their results and I could see the patterns that emerged, I then conducted another type of 360 survey, with Jacqueline's closest peers and senior management. I included Ben in this 360 survey. I did perceptual interviews to ask colleagues to reflect on working with Jacqueline over the past year. As I asked them questions about their recent interactions with her, they began to see for themselves how much she had grown and changed. One of her peers even said to me, "Wow, as I reflect on this conversation, I realize that, in the past six months, working with Jacqueline has been a pleasure. She listens and is more compassionate than I ever recall her being before. She is still focused on getting results, but she does it *with* people now, rather than talking *at* people. Jacqueline is now engaged in more authentic dialogue."

I asked Ben the same questions I asked the others, and he admitted that he had not worked with Jacqueline, or even taken the time to seek her out, in months. He was then interested to see the results of the 360 survey, so he could understand how people were experiencing working with Jacqueline now.

That is how Jacqueline changed her boss's perception of her abilities. And that is why Jacqueline was promoted into the role she really wanted—the role that suited her perfectly.

The specific feedback Jacqueline received from the 360 survey is very common. Perhaps you can see yourself or someone you know in this example.

If you want this type of feedback and you are not able to engage a coach to seek it out for you, I recommend you use this systematic way to discover your strengths and blind spots:

Make a list of the key stakeholders in your current role.

Make a list of the key stakeholders for the role you would like to have in the future.

Your goal now is to collect feedback from at least eight people about their experiences and perceptions of working with you. Even better would be to get feedback from ten or more people so you can see broader patterns. To do this you may create an anonymous survey, e-mail questions, or meet individually to ask questions that focus on the type of feedback you are seeking. Set up your expectations by talking with the person from whom you would like feedback. Say. "I've appreciated the opportunity to work with you, and I value your opinion. I'm focused on my own development and want to learn to be more effective in my role (or for a future role.) Would you be willing to share with me your thoughts on working with me? I have a survey or a few questions I'd like to ask you. When would you be available for this conversation?"

Customize the questions to your area of focus. Here are some examples of questions to consider for your survey or conversation:

In what ways have you seen me contribute to the organization? (You could also include team or product if that is your focus.)

What two or three words would you use to describe working with me?

What strengths do I bring to the team that you want to see me continue using?

What are my blind spots?

Is there anything you would like to see more of from me? Anything you would like to see less of from me?

What else do I need to know or understand about the business, culture, or future?

No matter what people say, thank each person for the feedback. Do not become defensive or try to explain why you did what you did in the past. Listen to the feedback and say, "Thank you."

Write a handwritten "thank-you" note to each person, indicating how much you appreciate that he or she was willing to participate in helping you.

Summarize all the feedback you receive in one report. Look at the themes. List the stories and examples you heard. Think about the impact of people's styles and motivators on how they experience working with you. Identify the possible interpretations of this cluster of information you collect.

Create a professional development plan for yourself. (You will find a free template for a professional development plan on my website at http://yourtalentatwork.com/learning-center /books/conversations-for-creating-star-performers-book/.) In this plan you will identify your top two or three areas for development and what specific actions you will take to develop them. You will find the 24 most important professional competencies and developmental actions for growing each in *Conversations for Creating Star Performers*.

For the next three to six months, focus on building the top two competencies that emerged from your list. You may want to keep your leaders aware of the specific actions you are taking to develop your capabilities as you go.

In six to twelve months, follow up with the people who provided you feedback. Ask what changes they have noticed. By doing this, you help them to recalibrate perceptions, based on their current experience in working with you. If the person you want to influence does not have a current experience working with you, then summarize what you have learned and how you are applying it to your current projects.

At this point you also may want to identify an additional eight to ten people and do the process again to see how your developmental focus has changed what others experience. This gives you a benchmark to compare your abilities now to what they were a year ago.

## In Action: Teresa Bryce Bazemore

Teresa Bryce Bazemore is the president of Radian Guaranty, Inc. She told me about an earlier time in her career, when she was the general counsel and corporate secretary involved in a start-up company. Initially, the founders of the start-up had a clear vision: they wanted to create a mortgage company with state-of-the-art technology to make the mortgage process smooth and efficient. Many mortgage companies at that time had legacy software that caused inefficiencies and too much paperwork.

The initial business plan included helping other companies provide state-of-the-art mortgage services to their existing clients in a cobranded model. However, after the sales team of the start-up began talking with prospective clients, it became apparent that prospective clients wanted a private label mortgage service to take over their existing mortgage operations. This new information caused the leadership team members to challenge each other's thinking; they had to ask lots of questions and push their assumptions, and they had to listen deeply. They had to work through the conflict of letting go of their original vision for building the company and segment the services differently. Teresa told me: "We had the technology team that was responsible for building a state-of-the-art mortgage platform and we had the

109

investors. Both groups spoke different languages—they had very different experiences. We realized you have to be really clear about what you want to build, how you want to get there, and what the requirements for success will be—these are not automatically understood by the various stakeholders. The technologists and the bankers always spoke different languages. Different things motivated each group. As we listened to each other and challenged each other's thinking, people began to get inspired about a new common vision. We saw the value in what other points of view could bring to the table. I'm a big believer in conversations for exploring new possibilities where you say, 'what should we be spending our time on? Are the things we are doing going to take us there? What do we need to be doing today? Do we have the right resources?' This is the kind of listening and collaborating that creates positive results."

## Tying People Reading Together Application Exercises

### Exercise 1: Connie's Dilemma

Imagine Connie is a colleague of yours. She comes to talk with you about a dilemma she is having at work. This is what she says:

"I have a peer, Lukas, who is very straightforward. He gives me constant feedback about how I am doing. Lately I find myself feeling annoyed when I know I am going to be meeting with Lukas, because he comments critically on my work every time

Worksheet to Practice People Reading in Meetings

Interaction: e.g., internal meeting, client meeting, one-on-one

My intended outcome:

| Participants | DISC Style Needs | Motivators Needs | Emotion Expressed | How I'll Respond |
|---|---|---|---|---|
|  |  |  |  |  |
|  |  |  |  |  |
|  |  |  |  |  |
|  |  |  |  |  |

we are together. He is in Germany and I am in one of our U.S.-based offices, so most of our conversations are by phone or e-mail.

"When I think about his communication style, I think he has a preference for High Dominant with a Compliant-to-Standards backup style. My own style is High Dominant with an Influence backup. From my observations, Lukas is motivated by Theoretical and Utilitarian values. I am motivated by Social and Traditional values.

"We have the same position, and there are many overlaps in our work. Our boss expects us to work together daily and pass projects back and forth as needed. We have the same technical expertise and goals. I want very much to be able to take his feedback positively, but I get triggered into defensiveness now whenever I hear his voice. If he suggests alternative ways of doing something, I feel annoyed and resentful. I believe he thinks what I do is not good enough.

"Recently he told me all my e-mails are 'full of agony and irritation' and that I am not a good communicator. He does not like it when I express emotion. How can I be more effective with him?"

Based on what you have learned so far, what would you say to Connie if she shared this with you? Formulate your reply to Connie.

### Exercise 2: Ellen's Story

Six months ago, Ellen moved to a new city to take what she thought would be her dream job: director of human resources. She dreamed about building a community of people around her with whom she would enjoy cocreating amazing experiences. With great excitement, she dove into her new role, eager to prove to her new boss, Juan, the chief financial officer, that he had made the right decision by hiring her.

Highly motivated to help people, Ellen works tirelessly on gathering information and research to help others' causes. Although she does not often advocate for herself, Ellen speaks up directly for others who can't speak for themselves. For this reason, Ellen is known for being direct, sometimes even too blunt.

Demonstrating strong financial results motivates Juan; he has a set of key performance indicators that he calls his "dashboard of data" that he uses to show progress in his monthly reports. Juan also wants to be seen as a leader who can solve complex problems. He prefers working on his own or one-on-one with another person as needed. He communicates most often in short, detail-oriented e-mails. He prefers consistent activities, never wants to be surprised, likes lots of time to make decisions, and seems to avoid variety in his day-to-day schedule.

Ellen works nonstop because she claims she is new in this town and has no friends or family nearby. However, when I looked into her history, I discovered that she has kept up a non-stop pace through most of her career, long before she moved into this new role. She has been working 15-hour days for the past few weeks, and now she is on overload.

Although Juan acknowledges that he does not have expertise in HR, according to Ellen, he is extremely critical of everything she is doing. He keeps rewriting her work, nitpicking over one word after another. This is emotionally draining and causes Ellen to feel that her boss shows her no respect. Ellen also claims that Juan leaves the office around 5 p.m. every evening after "dumping several hours of more work" on her. Ellen stays until 8 or 9 p.m. every night trying to get everything done. She wants so much to be acknowledged for her effort and the impact she is having.

Ellen is exhausted when she calls me on a Sunday morning. She is not sleeping well and is worried about her work relationships. Repeatedly, she tells me how she cannot get her boss to respect her contributions. Ellen describes several recent examples where she had an emotional hijacking and behaved harshly out of anger. It is clear to me that Ellen is stuck in a story. Ellen repeats the same story again: "He is not listening. He does not understand the value I bring to the role. I am afraid and don't know how to get the attention I need to move my projects forward." Ellen tells me she has worked all weekend and feels she must work all day on Sunday to prepare for a presentation on Monday.

After listening to Ellen describe her situation, I begin my response by asking her a question that will raise a mirror, so she can really see herself and the decisions she is making: "Today is Sunday; can you go for a long walk through the park today, eat a healthy meal, and then take a long nap?" Ellen replies: "No, I have not had a day off in weeks, but every hour of this day is already spoken for. I have to prepare slides for tomorrow's presentation to the executive team, go over every part of the Excel worksheet that will be given out, and . . . I have to work hard to get their attention!" Ellen goes on with a list that has 20 items on it. It is obvious to me that she is no longer thinking clearly, so I say: "Ellen, you can't perform at your best if you are exhausted. When was the last time you gave a great presentation while feeling overwhelmed and exhausted? That does not happen, and you are probably going to create a bigger problem for yourself by not taking care of your body, mind, and spirit first. Today needs to be about your resting, eating healthy food, and reminding yourself of why you do this work. What is meaningful about what you are doing?" Ellen replies, "My boss does not care if I did not have a weekend. He wants this presentation and the list done, and expects it to be e-mailed to him tonight."

What are Ellen's motivators?

Ellen's motivators are Social, Theoretical, and Utilitarian. Ellen's Social motivator can be seen in her willingness to work tirelessly for causes that benefit others. Since she likes to help people by researching and collecting information that suggests the presence of a Theoretical motivator. The clue to Ellen's third motivator is in her work history. While Ellen's new position is pushing her to her limits, she has worked at a nonstop pace for most of her career, which indicates a strong Utilitarian

113

motivator. The Utilitarian motivator drives her to complete projects and get results, but it also sets up an internal conflict, because people with this kind of motivator need a way to keep score and demonstrate significant progress. So while the Social motivator drives her to help others with no regard for getting something in return, her Utilitarian motivator demands a return on every investment of time, energy, and money. Her top two motivators—Social and Utilitarian—create a me-me conflict in Ellen, pulling her in different directions.

What are Juan's motivators?
Juan's motivators are Utilitarian, Individualistic, and Theoretical. His Utilitarian motivator can be seen in the fact that strong financial results are an incentive for him. That he wants to be seen as a leader (Individualistic) who can solve complex problems (Theoretical) demonstrates how his Individualistic and Theoretical motivators interact together.

What is Ellen's preferred communication style?
Ellen's preferred communication style is High Dominant with Influence as the next style.

Ellen's bluntness is a clue that she prefers the Dominant style. Also, her track record of working extremely hard and her willingness to keep working on the weekend show that she often operates from the Dominant style with Utilitarian motivators.

What is Juan's preferred communication style?
Juan's preferred communication style is equal parts of Compliant-to-Standards and Steady.

Juan prefers a Steady communication style as evidenced by his desire for consistency, dislike of change and surprises, need for time to make decisions, and criticism of other people's work. The fact that he is very set in his ways and detail-oriented points to his preference for the Compliant style as well.

What are the issues that will emerge as a result of the differences between their preferred communication styles?

There are many possible challenges based on their communication styles. Ellen's Dominant style is across the communication-style wheel from Juan's Steady style. Also, Ellen's Influence style is across the wheel from Juan's Compliant-to-Standards style. They are basically the complete opposite of each other when it comes to communication styles. Juan's criticism of Ellen could be from his discomfort with the pace at which she is moving or with the new direction she is moving in that is different from his modus operandi.

What would you advise that Ellen and Juan do to work well together?

Juan should explain to Ellen how he would like things done, but not overwhelm her with his criticism. If he explains clearly upfront what he would like, then he should not have to nitpick Ellen's work. Juan needs to realize that Ellen is the expert in her field and that he needs to give her some authority—allow her Dominant needs to be met with the decision-making responsibility for her role. Ellen needs to do work that is meaningful and innovative, but give Juan a chance to adjust and not push the limits too much.

Based on what you have just learned about Juan and Ellen, what kind of overtures should Ellen make to get Juan to explain things clearly up front and to recognize her as an expert in her field?

## Advanced People Reading

Now it is time for you to begin using all the parts of people reading together. First, begin to notice what communication style is showing up in a conversation or meeting. Then look at which motivators are being rewarded by the focus of the conversation or meeting. Finally, examine the emotional undertone in the conversation or meeting. How can you use this information to create positive outcomes? What does this mean for your "That's for Me!" list?

Practice people reading every day for the next 60 to 90 days, until doing this becomes automatic for you.

# PART 2

# THE BUILDING BLOCKS FOR SUCCESSFUL COLLABORATIONS THAT GET RESULTS

# CHAPTER 6

# Deep Listening

## What We Hear and What We Don't Hear: Learning to Listen

Imagine that you have never heard about or seen flowers. You are walking through a garden for the first time. What do you see? Can you see a tulip? If you do not know what a tulip is, you cannot see a tulip. What you may see are colorful things that are pretty. So if I said to you, "please bring me the tulip," would you know what to do? No. Would you have listened? You might have heard the request and the word "tulip," but you could not act on it because there was no understanding of what it meant. Only when you were shown a tulip would you be able to listen to, "please bring me a tulip" and know to go pick one. The more distinctions you have, the better you can hear what is being said.

Assuming that you heard the same thing as everyone else at a meeting or in a conversation is a mistake. Not hearing or not listening causes conflicts. Whenever someone who is a stakeholder in our work thinks, "He does not value me and my thinking enough to make time to hear my ideas," conflict is inevitable.

My grandmother was one of seven sisters. I recall listening as these seven sisters argued over whose version of a story was accurate. I was perplexed at the time about why they had very different versions of the same events. How could this be? Years later, as I sat at a conference table listening to several of my peers describe the task our boss had given us, I was reminded of my grandmother and her sisters, and found myself perplexed again. We had all heard the same directive, and yet we did not understand it the same way. We argued over what we were supposed to be creating, even though we had all heard the same message *at the same time.* How could this be?

When we have different communication styles and motivators driving our behavior, and when we are subject to our own unique patterns of emotions, we hear things differently. We may see the same visuals and listen to the same words at a meeting, but we will hear and understand them differently, because we use our own communication styles as our listening modes. For example, a person who prefers the High Dominant style will listen for results first, next actions, power, and competency. A person with a High Influence style will listen for creative ideas, emotions, what is popular, and opportunities to have fun. A person with a High Steady style will listen for how things will be done, ways to serve and please others, and will prefer listening to talking. Someone with a High Compliant style will listen for facts, details, data, logic, and research. When we do not understand these differences, misunderstandings occur, because we have different wiring connections in our brains.

Your workplace motivators, communication style, current emotion, and past experience determine what you do and don't hear. If you do not understand the communication styles model we discussed earlier, it will be difficult for you to pick out underlying needs in a conversation, just as it would be difficult to pick a tulip if you did not know what one looks like. Table 6.1 summarizes what people with each communication style listen for.

**TABLE 6.1** Identifying What People with Each Style Listen For

| High Dominant: Listens for results | High Influence: Listens for creative ideas | High Steady: Listens for process | High Compliance: Listens for facts |
|---|---|---|---|
| Next steps | Emotions | How to serve others | Details |
| Power | What's popular | How to please others | Logic |
| Competency | Opportunities for fun | Others' ideas before speaking | Research |

Most people are so habituated into their own ways of communicating and valuing experiences that they miss much of what goes on around them. They have not learned to hear or see from other perspectives. Have you noticed that the world is getting bigger for you, now that you are people reading? You now have more to see and hear in experiences with other people. You can now metaphorically distinguish tulips, roses, and daffodils from each other and pick the right one when asked to.

When attending a meeting with someone using the communication style directly across the wheel from you, notice that you may use the same words to mean different things. The word "research" means something different to someone who has a High Compliant style than it does to someone with a High Influence style. For example, when a High Compliant style communicator says, "I've researched this topic," she means that she has looked at ALL the relevant facts, articles, data, and put them together to see the whole picture. However, when a High Influence style communicator says, "My research tells me this is a good direction for us to move forward in," he means he found an article or saw a sign that caused him to feel like this was worthy of moving forward; he did not read every article, book, and report on the topic. He used his gut to make decisions, not necessarily facts and data. Clearly, these two types of communicators have very different understandings of what "research" means.

This is why it is so important for teams, departments, and companies to create their own language—to establish what is meant by the word "tulip" or "research." Creating a common language can directly influence the culture you create in your team, department, and organization.

The communication style model you learned earlier is a universal language; it works in every culture. Wherever you find human beings, you will also find communication styles and group dynamics affecting their behavior. Now you have new distinctions to hear and see what is happening in and around you. Your self-awareness is increasing.

The Japanese have many words for collaborating. They have far more distinctions around the concept of collaborating and saving face than Americans do. Does it suggest that the Japanese understand more about types of collaboration, if they have so many words for it? Yes, they have more expectations about the interactions between people based on their roles than Americans tend to. If someone can identify not just a tulip, but many types of tulips, we begin to think of that person as a tulip expert. The deeper our distinctions, the more likely we are to have sophisticated expertise in that area.

## When Listening Is the Solution

Have you ever noticed that when you are attentively listening to someone talking about his passion, when you are truly being there for someone else who is completely present, it feels like energy is flowing? There is a different quality to the conversation; it is meaningful. You experience a hot-spot flare of energy. This is what I call "deep listening." It is as if you are connected to a live wire, because pure energy flows easily. When marinating in joy, passion, and excitement, you are creating more joy and passion. Have you noticed that emotions are contagious? And, that as you listen to someone else basking in an emotion, you begin to experience it too? Emotions spread. What you are feeling, I can sense in your words, body language, and tone of voice. You give off a vibe, based on your current emotional set point.

Listening to yourself and identifying the emotion you are experiencing is useful, so that you can use your internal emotional guidance system to make wise choices about your next actions. In order to do that, you have to have distinctions about the wiring in your own brain that triggers an emotion. Remember puppies in the office? If someone brings puppies into your office, what are you likely to feel? I would feel joy, because I love playing with puppies, but someone else who does not like puppies may feel frustrated because the puppies are distracting and annoying; he or she believes puppies are not supposed to be in the workplace. Our thought patterns and beliefs trigger emotions, which can also trigger conflict and shut down our listening ability.

Since you can choose what you focus your thinking on, you can choose the emotions you experience—if you learn to deeply listen to yourself you can process yourself through your emotions as they arise. When you deeply listen, you are able to get unstuck—move out of the deep freeze. I call this "processing yourself through your emotions." You can also help others release stuck emotions by listening and asking the right questions. There are specific actions that correspond to deep listening.

When a topic is complex, emotional, or controversial, or anytime you are communicating with a stakeholder in your work, such as a customer (either internal or external), use these deep listening steps in order:

1. First, maintain eye contact, hear the tone of voice, the words being used by the speaker, and observe the body language the person uses while speaking. Notice whether words, tone of voice, and the facial expressions are aligned. When these things are not aligned, the person is experiencing internal conflict with the issue being discussed.

2. Next, ask two or three questions that do not have a judgmental tone to them. This could sound like: "Hmm, that is interesting, would you tell me more? What else was happening at the time? How many people were involved? Wow, what were you feeling when that happened?" These questions show you are interested, and they enable you to build on what the speaker has said already. (Asking questions like this will take you out of being reactive or defensive.)

3. When the speaker stops talking, allow a long pause, then summarize what you have heard so far and confirm you got it right. "What I've heard you saying is . . . XYZ. Have I heard you correctly?" or "You seem to be feeling . . . have I got that right?" Include both the content and the feeling tone of what you heard. Watch for a nod indicating that you heard correctly. The other person may jump in to add missing details. (Now the other person feels heard.)

4. After doing the first three steps, share your own thinking, observations, insights, and suggestions. Make your proposal, ask for what you want, or share what you are doing. (This is deep listening in action.)

Whenever someone shares something that shows vulnerability, emotion, or compassion, use these listening action steps. Also, when someone shares something complex or challenging, something that you need to understand so you can take action, use these steps. Master these behaviors so they are automatic, and they will then be there when you sense conflict and need to find resolutions as well.

We can learn to deeply listen to ourselves, to other individuals such as the boss, and to teams.

## Listening to Yourself

Do you pride yourself on being highly task focused? The downside to being highly task focused is that, instead of checking in to ensure you are focused on what brings joy, passion, and love to life, you get in a rat-race feeling, like being on a wheel spinning to nowhere. An overfocus on a task will lead to burn out, because we eventually realize our actions are not connected to our bigger goals or our motivators, and they do not trigger joy. This pattern is a sign that careful listening is missing from your relationship with yourself. If you do not have a habit of deeply listening to yourself, then it will also be very difficult to be present for others.

Your "That's for Me!" list and your learning journal are the first steps in listening to yourself. If you realize that you have not been present to your own needs, wants, goals, and dreams lately, it is time for some personal listening. I encourage each of my coaching clients to create a learning journal. This is a private conversation with yourself in which you summarize what you are experiencing as you are learning new things. By keeping a learning journal, you listen to yourself and track your own growth and development as you mature. You are better able to celebrate your accomplishments and growth, because you can review your journal and see your progress.

You begin to connect the dots and to experience deeper fulfillment by listening carefully to yourself first, and then to others. You also begin to see more clearly what you want to be committed to when you create a habit of listening to yourself. Your "That's for Me!" list can be included in your learning journal too.

## Are You Committed to Being a Great Listener?

When we have thought patterns that are a justification for not giving 100 percent of ourselves to the cause, to the team, to the mission, we need to see the core issue is a missing conversation with ourselves drawing out our real commitment. Somewhere a conversation for distinguishing commitment with ourselves has been glossed over, not explored, or ignored. What are you really committed to? It takes deep listening to yourself to know the answer to this question. Time to go back to your "That's for Me!" list. Is being a great listener on your list?

Are you ready to be known as a great listener? You have to admit who you are, what you really want, and with whom you want to work. When it is not clear what you are committed to creating in your work, in your career, and in your business relationships, then habitual negative thinking takes over. Ignored, this negative thinking can continue automatically. But if you tune in and begin to hear it in your private thinking, then you can alter it. This is the root of deciding who you want to be and what you are committed to. When you learn how to deeply listen to yourself, you can invent who you want to be in your work and in your life; you can create what you want and inspire yourself to take actions that align with what you really want. Your "That's for Me!" list will reflect who you are and what you are committed to creating, because you listen to yourself and guide your emotions intentionally.

If you take on a commitment to produce a new result at a level far beyond what you do now, then you become bigger—your focus expands. For this to happen, you have to make a commitment for your own growth. Carefully listening to yourself is what it takes in order to recognize the areas in which you would be willing to make a bigger impact than you are now. What is a goal you'd like to commit to—perhaps something on your "That's for Me!" list that will expand your focus and require you to collaborate on a larger scale? Notice your repeated thoughts and observe the effect they have on how you interact with others and your ability to expand your focus.

## Your Beliefs Affect Your Listening

Do you enjoy listening to other people? Do you enjoy connecting with others to build relationships that encourage engagement and endorsement? Or are you more likely to think: "I already know what needs to be done. I get frustrated when I am talking to others, because they are too slow. They don't take the actions I want done in the way I know it needs to be done"? Or, "I am introverted and too shy to collaborate with others"?

A negative core thought is one that has a negative effect on what you believe. It does not support you. It is a thought you have that shows up over and over as a persistent complaint. It could be a thought about others or about yourself. Or it could be a thought that others have about you that prevents them from sharing with you. The negative story plot keeps repeating itself, if you do not realize you are the source of the story line. Not every thought you have is the truth.

Have you listened to yourself recently? What are the things you think about most? These are some common thought patterns that get people into trouble in connecting with others:

She does not listen to me.

I'm not good enough.

I don't know how to do this, and I don't think I can learn it.

He is too slow in his speaking, and I feel like I need to insert my ideas to get him moving.

He does not care about what I am doing.

No one notices the contributions I am making.

I do not have enough of what I want. I'm overwhelmed, with too much to do.

I want to be a part of a high-performing team, but I can't find one.

She does not respect me. I feel like I have to beg for attention from her.

What you think others are thinking about you may also have a negative effect on you. Do any of these sound familiar?

My coworkers think I make decisions too quickly (or not quickly enough).

My employees believe that I lose myself in relationships with bosses and don't speak up for what I believe (or I push too hard for my own agenda without being aware of the effect on others).

Peers believe I am selectively honest, because I hesitate to share my thinking if I think people will disagree.

Others see me as stuck in fear (or anger, or sadness).

We cannot be in a conversation that focuses on complaining and be happy at the same time. Whining and judgmental thinking about others are signals that we are not happy. These negative thought patterns sabotage our ability to connect with people in meaningful conversations. So why do we do this? We do not see what we are doing when we make tradeoffs.

These tradeoffs happen behind the scenes in our thinking. They are so habitual that we do not notice them. These thoughts are like a security blanket that keeps us from being fully present to ourselves and others.

It is likely that the pathways for this type of thinking were laid down in our brains when we were very young. These are some examples:

- We get to be right at the expense of making the other person wrong, instead of authentically partnering and possibly apologizing for our part in a mistake.
- We avoid taking responsibility, thus preventing us from being able to take on the next huge project.
- We dominate others with our thinking and misery, instead of processing ourselves out of our stuck emotions and inspiring growth and forward momentum.

- We make others suffer with us, so we do not feel alone, instead of stepping up and creating what we really want and collaborating in an inspiring manner.
- We rationalize for our current situation: "It is not my fault!" We feel justified with the situation by blaming someone else, instead of creating game-changing moments that build breakthrough results.

Negative behaviors and outcomes result from repeated negative thoughts. Conversely, a cooperative, collaborative mindset emerges as a result of positive self-fulfilling thoughts. These thinking habits guide you toward cooperation or competition. Then your capacity and willingness to guide others within your organization creates a sense of shared purpose, mutuality, and collegiality. This is all based on what you think. Have you listened to yourself lately on these issues? What is your shared purpose with the people you interact with most? How does mutuality and collegiality play out in those relationships? If you can't answer these questions quickly, take time to explore them in your learning journal. Then begin to ask and speak about them in your conversations with others.

What enables us to change our limited thought patterns into more positive thought patterns? We will release our habitual way of thinking when one or more of these occurs:

The cost of our stinking thinking gets so intense that we cause a crisis (like being fired or losing an important relationship due to a bad attitude) and we decide we have to change.

We practice deep listening with ourselves and others daily until it becomes a way of being.

We intentionally develop our emotional intelligence and learn how to use each of the seven core emotions— operating much of our time from the top emotions.

We are diligent about paying attention to what we are thinking and feeling in the moment, so we can make choices instead of reacting automatically as if on an automatic pilot.

Be courageous enough to look at your own thought patterns. Noticing your own flawed thinking enables you to rewire the thoughts and beliefs that do not serve you. You can then create breakthrough thinking and results. The ability to do this begins with listening, to ourselves first, and then to others.

## Listening to Another Person

Being fully present to another person because you are clear about who you are and what you are bringing into a conversation feels great. When you believe this, you will begin to measure your success each day by how often you carefully listen to what is happening in your interactions with others in the moment. Are you fully present in the moment now? Some people measure a day's successes by how many tasks were completed, how many check marks show up on the to-do list. When you do this, you are likely missing the soft skills or the people dynamics; you miss the dance, because you are so focused on the next action. Do you have on your list measuring success by how many times you felt connected to the person with whom you were talking? Is being connected in a meaningful way something you track?

If we have not been deeply listening to others or if we are known as someone who does not listen well because we are so focused on results and actions and evaluating competencies in the moment, it is time for a change. Practice the listening steps intentionally in every conversation for the next 30 days. If we have a bad habit of interrupting others, having our body language indicate that we are ready to speak while the other person is still speaking, then we need to be aware of when this is happening. Sit peacefully. Take deep breaths as the other person is speaking, and calm your mind. Have a pleasant facial expression. Ask thoughtful questions that build on what was said. Share your experience, observations, and insights as someone who is collaborating in a partnership, not dictating the only right or possible path.

There is a big difference between telling someone what to do and engaging him or her in new thinking that creates new results and learning. Both of these options occur in conversations; it is the quality of the listening that makes the difference. Imagine that a conversation is like playing catch the ball. In tossing the ball back and forth, you can catch it and respond, drop it, or ignore it as if it never existed. You do this hundreds of times every day when interacting with others.

Assignment: Practice listening to people with no judgment, criticism, or internal conflict while they are speaking. Notice their styles and motivators without judging them. Listen and observe as others are speaking, and notice when you are not able to listen deeply. In your learning journal, record the times when you are able to intently listen, as well as the patterns that are occurring when you are not able to. How can you create more moments where you are deeply listening to yourself and others?

## Listening to a Team

Marjorie had an unconscious way of being that was habitually busy and in a hurry when she met with her team. Marjorie was committed to producing results. She was known as a go-getter who could make things happen. Marjorie regularly told others what to do and asserted her point of view in her conversations. She had never made a commitment to being a great listener. As a result, she often unknowingly squashed other people's creativity and conversations for exploring new possibilities.

Marjorie's preferred communication style is Dominant with Influence as a backup. Her top workplace motivators are Utilitarian and Theoretical. She wants to get things done and be seen as highly competent and efficient. Marjorie likes provocative discussions that challenge the status quo. She is also frequently going back and forth between fear that others are not performing to her standards or anger that something has crossed her boundaries. Thus others felt like she was not listening or present in the moment; they saw her as always striving for some future desired results and as a know-it-all. Being too busy can be a wall that prevents real listening from occurring. It also prevents collaborations that can enable growth. Have you ever observed this pattern in someone like Marjorie?

Have you noticed that what you want to listen to when you are in team meetings aligns with your own goals? Can you make your goals broad enough so you are interested in whatever your peers are accomplishing, so you want to listen to their perspectives when they speak in team status meetings?

Do you believe that profit is the measure of success in business? Some people do and others do not. Your values determine how you will measure success. What is the measure of success in your business and on your team? Your answer to this question highlights what you will want to listen to. The whole game of business and organizational culture consists of goals and rules that revolve around a values hierarchy.

In an organization where I work with the senior leadership team, they have a common language that sounds like this:

Make a profit or you can't stay in business.

Know your profit numbers every day; they are the final score at the end of each year.

Be an expert in our products and services.

Deliver what you promise in the most efficient ways possible.

Work hard and smart to get the business.

Generate new business in order to grow.

Keep your suppliers happy, so they keep supplying you efficiently and provide knowledge updates quickly.

Commit to being the best in delivering useful services and products.

This organization has High Utilitarian, Theoretical, and Individualistic values. As a result, when working with this leadership team, effective team members listen and speak to ideas and suggestions that align with these common goals.

What happens when a team culture changes? Perhaps a new boss has been assigned to lead the team, and that person has another value at the top of her list. Say Social is now in the top with Utilitarian. Now the new goals include being collaborative and consultative in working together productively. This shift affects the way listening and speaking occur in team meetings.

What are the agreements you and your team use to measure your success? With your team, is being collaborative more important than being individually results oriented? Or are they both equally important in the way your team operates? How does this affect what you listen to now?

We measure what is important to us. What do we track to demonstrate our results? Some businesses track the following:

Gross sales: total dollar amount sold

Expenses: what is spent

Customers: number of people served

Sponsors: number of people who endorse the company

New customers: number of new customers this month

Receivables: what is owed—the total of all outstanding invoices

Payables: what is owed to others

Gross profit or loss

Revenue: total income

Checking balance: current cash on hand

Make sure your team members—the people you want to collaborate with—are crystal clear about what you are listening for in order to track results. Say to them, "You will get my attention easily when you focus on _____. Use these key words and you will be able to get my attention." By giving people clarity about how to gain your attention, you avoid the perception that it is hard to get your attention or that you do not listen to what is important.

Leaders also need to clarify how often we want to look at each measurement as a team. Some numbers may be weekly, while others may be monthly. Our expectations around this affect what we are listening for when we meet.

What would we track if we wanted to increase sales and growth? How about the following?

Number of new sales contacts

Number of appointments to create conversations for new possibilities

Number of conversations with current customers

Number of phone conversations with prospects to schedule in-person meetings

Number of referrals

Would tracking these numbers affect what we were listening for? If you were on a team that wanted more sales growth, you would be wise to listen for these things and be prepared to speak about them. People would listen to your ideas if you framed them with this context.

## Stuart's Story

Stuart Hacker is responsible for talent management at the pharmaceutical company Sanofi. He and his team created a program called "Talking Talent" because they wanted to engage people in conversations focused on talent development. They wanted to provide people with a forum to hear each other and to confirm common understanding of the messages. The intent of the program is to gather human resources business partners together on a consistent basis to discuss talent and explore opportunities to proactively share across the region. This process gets people on the same page, hearing the same message at the same time. To ensure that the people who were invited to the program understood what was involved, Stuart created a structure and put it into a one-page overview of the project to help them focus their speaking and listening during the meeting. The following is the communication outline Stuart created to get people on the same wavelength about the purpose and emphasis of the collaboration so they could focus their listening:

### Talking Talent Meetings
- Who will attend
  - **The core group:** This group is responsible for communicating and getting information for the meeting.
  - **Topic sponsor:** The person who is responsible for the topic or talent that will be discussed.

- **Staffing and HR:** Business partners (HRBP) who are affected by or can support the topics or talent that will be discussed at the meeting.
- Topics to discuss
  - **Key open positions:** Staffing shares key open positions and elicits any future open positions.
  - **Developmental positions:** Determine positions that would perfect developmental opportunities for early potentials.
  - **"Talent Spotlight" discussion:** HRBP leads share a specific talent who is ready for a move and/or additional developmental opportunities.
- To help in selecting the talents you would like to showcase, ask these questions about them:
  - Are they potential leaders?
  - Can they move to new locations within the United States?
  - Have they been in their roles for more than 12 months?
- You also need to consider various "hot topics"—critical topics and future trends that may affect your talent pool and influence future trends.
- Further, you need to consider how the members of the core group responsible for an activity or business will determine who will be included, the topic, and the individuals they would like to spotlight.
- Talent management and staffing will create the agenda and set up the meeting logistics.

Stuart gleaned something important from this experience about collaborating: "Creating the time and space for our HR leaders to come together, to talk with each other in a focused conversation, caused us to listen to each other and proactively collaborate on talent topics at Sanofi. It enabled us to provide greater visibility to our talent, provide solutions to pressing concerns each leader had, and created greater movement for our talent across all our businesses. Listening and collaborating like this is paying off in measurable ways." Creating a forum focused on a specific topic and pulling people out of their normal routines so they can listen to the same message at the same time is important, especially when the volume of work and change going on overwhelms everyone. Give people clear directions, confirm they have received the same message and understand it, and then give them the time to collaborate together focused on the intention of the communication. That is what Stuart did that created positive results.

## The Team Member, Peer, or Boss Who Never Listens!

I am frequently asked what to do when the boss, colleague, or staff members seem as if they are not listening to what is most important to you. It can sound like this: "What do I do when my colleague is not willing to collaborate with me? He barks orders and then is gone." Or it may sound like this: "How can I get my boss's attention? She is chronically busy and seems so overwhelmed and focused on tasks that I do not feel like we ever have conversations to explore ideas and new possibilities together. We are not connected." Or another version. "He nods, smiles, seems friendly during our conversations, and then afterwards it is as if we never discussed the topic at all. No action is taken on what we discuss."

The first step, no matter which role you are in, is to ask for time together to have a conversation for connection. I frequently advise people to set up meetings with their bosses, team members, or colleagues outside the normal office space, so that they can be present to each other without the distractions of the office. Make a point to say, "I am turning off my phone so I can be completely present with you in this conversation." By saying this, I am making a commitment, and I want the other person to do the same. These are signals that we are ready to connect, collaborate, and respect each other's input.

When someone seems like he is not listening to you, say this with a calm supportive tone of voice and a kind facial expression:

"You seem preoccupied, would you like me to come back at another time? I'll get out my schedule so we can find a time when we will be able to listen to each other." Ask people, "Is now a good time for us to be able to listen to each other?" If someone still looks uninterested in what you are communicating, check out your interpretation by saying: "It looks like you may not be interested, but I wanted to be certain. Am I interpreting that correctly?"

If you have tried repeatedly to ask for listening and connection in a relationship with a boss, peer, or team member and you still feel like you are not getting it, then what? Whenever you are faced with a person or people who don't seem willing to listen or collaborate, but prefer to bully, you have choices about how to handle this. You always have choices!

Let's consider some of your choices as an employee:

1. You can stay and be miserable, bitter, and resentful. Focus on the long-term problems and differences in your styles and motivators. Make others wrong for not being like you.
2. You can stay and be happy. Shift within you what you are focused on. Learn to play to the strengths of others' motivators and styles. Learn to process yourself and others through stuck emotions.
3. You can leave and be resentful about being pushed out. Become bitter, angry, and resentful, because the other person did not appreciate your style and motivators.
4. You can leave, learn the lessons from your feelings, and choose a better path for yourself that aligns with your preferred communication style, motivators, and "That's for Me!" list.

Now let's consider some of your choices when you are the leader. There are four reasons why people do not take the action you want them to:

1. They do not know what you want them to do.
2. They do not know how to do it.
3. They do not want to do it.
4. They are incapable of doing it.

The solution to an employee not knowing what you want him to do is communication—talk through the role, clearly define each action and the desired outcome. Ask questions to confirm understanding and listen to how the employee will apply and act on your conversation.

The solution to an employee not knowing how to do what you want done is training that sets the foundation for her thinking and behaviors related to achieving the goal. Show the employee how to do it and what the desired finished product looks like. Then provide development feedback day-to-day for the next 30 days as she practices obtaining the desired results herself.

The solution, if an employee does not want to do it, is to have a motivation-focused conversation about his values and workplace motivators. Talk through the positive and negative consequences of not doing it, for the individual and for the organization. Help him to make a conscious decision about his own motivation for the task. Highlight the rewards that come from the nature of the work itself.

The solution, if an employee is incapable of doing it, is to have her clearly see that there is a role mismatch—as if we are trying to put a square peg in a round hole.

You will not know if someone is incapable until you have ensured that possibilities 1–3 were covered. Once you know for sure these possibilities were properly addressed, the employee will understand that he or she needs to move into another role that is a better fit for his or her strengths and current capabilities.

The value in learning how to deeply listen, so that employees get unstuck and back on track, is as valuable as gold. As a manager or team leader, you serve a very specific purpose for the person you are developing; your role is to inspire and instruct others to achieve their goals and improve the business. If you do not inspire them to get unstuck and have clarity about the next steps to take to get on the right track, you are not performing your role. Become an inspiration for other people to achieve what they want to achieve. To reignite in yourself and others the passion to grow and to move forward, you must be a great listener.

## When Others Are Trying to Get You to Listen

Do you notice when someone is working hard to get your attention?

Why is it important for you to listen to others? Engagement and meaning in relationships relies on high-quality listening. People do not buy your ideas or take action on your orders solely because of what you say. They buy your ideas because of how you listen to them and how you apply what you have learned from listening to them. This is a key to engagement. Great listening is being there without judgment of the other person's style, motivators, or current emotion. This type of listening has a transformational quality to it. Most of us have been taught how to speak clearly, but not how to listen carefully in order to engage in conversation. It takes practice to become a masterful listener.

## In Action: Adam Berman

Adam Berman is currently the president of the board of the Philadelphia Human Resources Planning Society (PHRPS) and practice leader at Kreischer Miller. Kreischer Miller is an independent accounting, tax, and advisory firm. This firm is known for responding to the unique needs of private companies, helping them smoothly transition through growth phases, business cycles, and ownership changes.

When I asked Adam what was it about his background that made him an effective leader, he told me about his first leadership role, when he was promoted to team leader reporting to the president. The people who now reported to Adam were his former peers. Each was far more experienced and older than he was. Some of Adam's new staff members, like Roger, had 20 years more experience in working in this organization than Adam did, and all of them were already experts in running their departments. Adam felt intimidated and terrified the first time he had to lead a team meeting, and it showed in his body language, tone of voice, and the way he overfocused on tasks and not on listening.

After the first team meeting, Roger approached Adam and said: "Adam, you may not know this, but we told the president we wanted you in this role because we knew you would be a good listener and facilitator. I've never seen you terrified like you were today in our team meeting. All you have to do is do what you did before you were the leader. Take your ego out of the room, listen to the whole message, then marshal every resource you can to help each person meet his goals. Everyone wants you to succeed, and you will, when you do the things you were doing before you were promoted." After this conversation with Roger, Adam reached out to another of the team members, Pat, and asked her for her guidance. Pat said: "Listen to us individually and as a group. Poke holes in our thinking fearlessly AND with compassion, just as you did when you were our peer. Listen to everyone as a sounding board, and ask questions just like you did before." Adam then reached out to each of his new staff members and asked them, "What would you like from me in my new role?" Adam was listening.

As a result of these conversations, Adam realized people wanted him to be a sounding board, someone they could trust to help them achieve their goals. For him to succeed as a leader, he would need to listen carefully, without asserting his own agenda until after he fully listened to the whole message. As Adam explains: "I learned to separate what I wanted from the vision others were creating. I realized that asserting my will would derail others' passions, so I adapted my style to fit the needs of the moment. I let others do their jobs and saw it as my job to give the tools, resources, hugs, kicks in the butt, and whatever it was that would enable them to succeed in their goals. I had to fully understand their individual goals." This experience honed Adam's leadership capability.

Adam learned from his colleagues, and he also learned from his mistakes: "The times I failed were when I did not listen. Sometimes I did not allow others to do what they were best at doing, or I did not challenge them in areas when I sensed something was off." Evaluating his failures, changing his listening behaviors, and resuming his role as facilitator enabled Adam to successfully lead his team to be high-performing collaborators in running a major organization.

It is this collaborative leadership style that has enabled Adam to succeed in being the president of the board of PHRPS, a volunteer organization in which I felt lucky to serve with him and witness his ability to align team members to reach their goals together.

## Listening Application Exercise

Create a tracking system for your team, if you do not currently have key performance goals or a dashboard of measures, that you look at together regularly. Begin posting your team results. Make a commitment to knowing your results and creating conversations that highlight them to key stakeholders. Tell the people with whom you collaborate how to get your undivided attention.

Identify the people you spend the most time with. Rate on a scale of 0 through 10 the quality of listening that occurs in each relationship. What do you notice? Whom do you listen to most? Who is an outstanding listener for you?

Ask five people these questions:

What do I do as a listener that you want me to keep doing?

What do I do as a listener that you would like me to stop doing?

How do you experience conversations with me?

Notice where you need to adapt your communication and listening styles. I am frequently asked, "Who adapts to whom?" If you are an employee, do not expect your boss to adapt to your style. If you are a manager, do not expect your employees to adapt to your style. If you have the awareness that adaptation is needed to create effective communication and to be heard, then you take the responsibility to apply what you have learned so that you achieve the desired results. With whom will you be more aware of adapting your style? How could you work more effectively with your team, based on what you have learned?

For some of my coaching clients, this assignment is very challenging. As they describe how difficult it is for them, I am reminded of the butterfly's crucial struggle to escape its cocoon. The effort to break through the cocoon builds muscles in the butterfly's wings and legs, muscles that are critical for its survival. Similarly, as my clients struggle with this assignment, they too develop new skills and abilities. To avoid the struggle is to avoid the development that comes with it. In other words, no one can do the work for them; they have to learn how to listen to themselves, and then to others, in order to become effective communicators. In what ways do you notice yourself growing?

Is there someone with whom you struggle to get his or her attention so that you feel heard? If you want someone to listen to you, let him or her know you are listening. Create the right time and right space for a conversation that will enable listening with this person and practice what you have learned here.

Begin a learning journal, and pull out your favorite questions from this chapter to use as a starting point for writing in your journal.

Go back to your "That's for Me!" list. What do you want to measure and track regularly in order to demonstrate that you are moving forward? How could you share this with your peers, boss, and team, using language that will cause them to listen?

# CHAPTER 7

# Relationship and Group Dynamics That Affect Collaboration

Are you able to see relationships and group dynamics and understand how they will affect the interactions between people? Understanding relationship dynamics is the ability to see around the corner and prepare for what is coming next in an interaction with someone else or a group of people. Now I'm going to dive into what you need to know to see the patterns in people dynamics, so you can see around corners in collaborations with both individuals and groups. I'm going to give you new lenses to use when looking at groups. When we have a high level of awareness, we are able to be more effective collaborators. We are also able to become builders and leaders of high-performing teams.

## Partnership and Enmeshment

First, let's define the terms *partnership* and *enmeshment* as they relate to individual relationships.

A partnership relationship is what exists when two people decide to do something together, and they grow as a result.

Please hold both your hands up in front of you now, thumbs touching and fingers pointing to the ceiling. Wiggle your fingers up and move your hands up. Imagine each hand is a person and the wiggle up is the two people growing and making progress upwards together. Because they are nearby, sharing ideas, information, or a story, and because the two people are carefully listening and pointed in the same direction, they are growing together. The same dynamic can occur with a group of people in a partnership relationship together.

An enmeshed relationship is what exists when two people get so overly focused on each other that they lose focus on their common goal to grow and get results together. Please clasp your hands together, interlocking your fingers sideways. It is hard to move up or grow in this enmeshed dynamic. When partners are in an enmeshed relationship, they may each be so overly focused on what the other person is doing that they take their attention off their own "That's for Me!" lists. The blame game and passive-aggressive patterns emerge when enmeshed relationships occur. In enmeshed relationships, one person has an agenda he or she expects the other person to live according to.

You could be "partners" with a boss, a peer, a colleague, a parent, or even a child. I'm not using the word "partners" here to mean business partners or married partners, but rather to represent a way of growing together, focused on results, and collaborating. I use the word "partners" to describe a feeling that surrounds the way people interact with each other. If you are respectful of each other's "That's for Me!" lists, and if you find that some of the items on your separate lists align, you can grow and play together. You can focus on creating what you both want. Then you are in a partnership; then you are co-creating. Your group dynamic as it relates to accomplishing and experiencing could be called "being partners." This is necessary for engagement and healthy collaboration.

Let me share another way of thinking about partnership and enmeshment. Imagine we are in a huge kitchen. There are many of us in this amazing kitchen, each standing at our own cooking island. We can talk with each other as we prepare our own meals. Every type of ingredient is available to us. We've decided to come together to enjoy making our own pizzas. I am putting pineapple and pepperoni on my gluten-free pizza crust. Have you selected the meat-lovers delight with a thick crust? Or maybe you wanted mushrooms, garlic, and onions on a thin crust? Whatever you want, the choice is yours. There is no right or wrong way to prepare this meal. There is no judgment. You are experiencing total unconditional acceptance as you create your pizza. You are making your own choices, and so am I. We are both creating desired outcomes. We are being "partners" as we co-create this experience.

Now imagine that Patel comes over to my island in the kitchen and says, "You should not be having pepperoni on your pizza!" She starts removing the pepperoni from my pizza, even though I did not ask her to do so. Patel is enmeshed. She has lost focus on her own pizza, and she is now trying to fix mine to suit her agenda. I have choices about how I will respond to her. I can let her mess up my pizza, or I can tell her to get lost, this is my pizza. I do not want to enmesh with Patel, so I kindly send her on her way. I want to be partners, engaged in having fun and growing together. I do not want to make someone else's pizza or have her make mine. I want to be partners growing and experiencing life together in all my relationships.

## Decision-Making Power and Control

Now let me add another dimension to explore that has to do with power and control, especially in decision making. Do you share power and control in decision making, or is one person up and the other person down in the decision-making process? Does one person own the right to make the decision and do so *without* input from the other?

Do you discuss how decisions will be made together *before* decisions are made? If so, you are likely operating like partners and collaborating.

Imagine two stick figures standing next to each other on an equal level. We could say that these two stick figures represent being partners.

When we are in a shared partnership dynamic, we share power and control as we make decisions together as partners.

When we are in a one-up-one-down dynamic, one person owns the power and control and makes the decision without collaborating. One person is more powerful than the other and dictates what will be done. Imagine the two stick figures with one above the other representing one being on a higher level than the other. The lower figure reports into the higher figure.

Each of these patterns shows up frequently in the workplace.

Allow me first to give you an example that is not from the workplace, so that the implications from the business examples will be easier to understand. When I was a young girl, my father would sometimes announce, "There is something new in the driveway today!" My mother, sister, and I would race to the driveway to discover what new car my father had purchased. There was no discussion about what the new family car would look like. My father owned the decision, even though it affected all of us. My mother was always surprised by what her new car looked like. This decision-making process was classic one-up/one-down with my father being the owner of the decision.

This is the same dynamic that occurs when a supervisor says, "Here is the new assembly line that will replace the one you have been using," when there has been no prior discussion about a new assembly line being implemented—or even considered. Or when a peer announces in a presentation to your joint boss, "This is our proposal," indicating that it reflects suggestions from the team, though you had no input into what was created. This is not collaborating.

When you say, "Let's decide together *how* this decision will be made," you are likely collaborating in a partnership—you are cocreating a decision path. Decision making can be a joint responsibility.

If you habitually put yourself into the one-down position with others, deferring to them to make decisions, you are giving away your power and your ability to partner. They will feel like you are not taking initiative, and eventually they will lose respect for you. Instead, put yourself into a partnership and begin to cocreate how decisions will be made. Discuss up front how decisions will be made from a place of partnering.

Regarding the car-buying story: today, when my husband and I are considering buying a new car, or anything important, we do so together. We determine what the goal is, and we come up with options we both like that could meet the goal. Then we communicate with our children to explore their opinions about the options, and we enable them to propose additional options— illustrating to them that their voices matter in decision making. Even though my husband and I will make the final decision jointly, their input is considered. This same model of decision making applies at work when a client wants to build a curriculum for leadership in his or her organization. We approach it by collaborating on how key decisions will be made in the project. We are choosing partnership in decision making.

Each of these decision-making dynamics has pros and cons. Being able to spot the pattern you are in with someone or with a team is useful. Being able to talk about which style you want to use before a decision is made enables real partnerships to form. We might decide that, on the XYZ project, we will use partnership and on the PQR project you will take the lead.

Trust builds when we have these conversations and do what we agreed to in decision making.

As a leader, it is important to distinguish which type of decision making you expect the people who report to you to use with you and when. Michelle Staas and I work together. She owns the administration and office management for most things in our office, even though I own the company. Because I trust her and her decision-making ability in her job, every week when we meet for two hours, she is in the one-up position as she tells me what she needs from me. During that time she can delegate to me if needed. We have agreed she owns her projects. She is in the driver's seat, telling me what she has done or will do, delegating to me and asking me questions. We partner, even though I am the boss.

The decision about how we will move forward may be that Michelle will own the decision-making responsibility and I will trust and support her judgment. Sometimes Michelle and I agree that I will own the decision-making responsibility on a particular project, and other times we will co-own or jointly decide on something before moving forward. Using the earlier metaphor about pizza making, you could say we do not make each other's pizza. Pizza-making responsibilities are clearly defined in our conversations when we are in a healthy partnership dynamic. We decide together how we will make a decision about something, and we move forward with that plan.

When we feel powerless in our work or when we are living a victim story, there is no conversation about how decisions will be made. There is an automatic assumption that someone else will be making the decision. We are unhappy, shut down, in a bad habit or pattern of relationships that put us into the one-down role. That is a signal we need a more productive way of making decisions.

## Teresa's Group Decision-Making Story

Earlier we discussed Teresa Bryce Bazemore, the president of Radian Guaranty Inc. Teresa served on a non-profit board that produced breakthrough results because of the way board members partnered in decision making about what was important. The board asked the question, "What do we need to do to accomplish our vision?"

Teresa said: "We had a list that was too long for the resources we had available. We realized as a board we would have to prioritize the list of initiatives, because we could not be successful if we tried to do it all. We did not want people working to the point of exhaustion or getting overwhelmed, spinning on a wheel going nowhere, so we agreed we had to decide what to spend our resources on. To ease decision making and ensure we heard from each person, we did an activity we called, 'Spend the Dime.' We put a list of all the possible projects onto the wall of the boardroom. Each board member was given 10 pennies. We each had to allocate our 10 pennies. Some people taped all ten on one project and others spread theirs across several projects. At the end of the activity, it was clear which were the high priorities for us to focus our resources on, based on equal input from every board member. This activity enabled us to have effective discussions about each project and make sure we saw our joint priorities clearly together. This successful collaboration activity caused us to want more opportunities to work together. We produced amazing breakthroughs in our work as a result."

In Spencer Johnson's book, *"Yes" or "No": The Guide to Better Decisions*, he provides a map for better decision making:

## "Yes" or "No": The Map to Better Decisions

I avoid indecision and half decisions based on half-truths.

I use both halves of a reliable system to consistently make better decisions: a cool head and a warm heart.

I use my head by asking a practical question.

I consult my heart by asking a private question.

Then, after I listen to myself and then others, I make a better decision and act on it.

To use my head, I ask this practical question: Am I meeting the real needs, informing myself of options, and thinking it through? Yes _____ or No _____

Is it a mere want or a real need? What information do I need? Have I created options and discussed them with others? If I did "X" then what would happen? Then what?

To consult my heart, I ask a private question: Does my decision show I am honest with myself, trust my intuition, and deserve better? Yes _____ or No _____

Am I telling myself the truth? Does this feel right? What would I decide if I wasn't afraid? What would I do if I deserved better?

If "Yes," I proceed; if "No," I rethink.

What is my better decision?

I've used this decision-making map hundreds of times with teams to evolve thinking and come to a better decision than any one person would make on his or her own. The questions guide a great conversation, either individually or with groups.

When a person only uses one side of this decision-making model, it causes other people around him or her to overfunction in the other side. Let's look at Joe as an example. Joe uses the practical, logic questions when making decisions. He thinks through the options, and he decides based on what is most useful. He does not ask himself the warm heart questions. As a result, it often looks like fear or risk aversion is guiding his decisions. He does not take action on what he would love to do, or what would bring him joy. Joe is underfunctioning in the warm heart area. This causes the people who are closest to him to react by overfunctioning in the warm heart area when they are interacting with Joe. Have you ever observed this dynamic playing out in collaboration?

## Overfunctioning and Underfunctioning

One of the dynamics that often occurs when two people are enmeshed is that one begins to overfunction while the other underfunctions. Imagine this situation:

Tammy needs to fill an entry-level role in her company. Her college roommate's son Tom recently graduated from college and is not working. Tammy agrees to interview him for the job. In the interview process, Tom projects confidence, asserting that he is the right person for the role. He convinces Tammy and her team that he has a strong interest in this entry-level position. Tammy hires Tom and begins training him to fit into her company.

As part of his work, Tom commits to several key goals and a timeline for completing them. His project due dates slip, and he does not speak up to say there is a problem. Since Tom is nonchalant about the results and shows no sense of urgency to solve the issues he has created, it appears that he is not taking his work seriously. In addition to shirking his responsibilities, Tom asks for two weeks of vacation during the heavy workload.

Tammy begins to feel anxious whenever she sees Tom or thinks about the projects he is supposed to have already completed. Tammy calls Tom into her office and asks him for an update on what is happening. She adds, "It does not appear the results are coming together here, Tom. How can I be helpful?"

Tom seems to make up excuses and blame others for the situation he is in; he seems distracted and not engaged in solving the issues at hand by taking responsibility himself. He says he can't get himself focused, but that he will figure it out. Tom often works from an office in his home, as he does not have to work in the main office. A week goes by, and then another, and it still seems as if nothing is moving forward with Tom, but he does not say anything about this. Tammy then asks if Tom needs her to manage his daily schedule for him. He shrugs his shoulders, rolls his eyes, and says he is having a hard time getting up in the mornings. As a result, Tammy starts to call his home each morning. She says she wants to, "Wake him up and get him moving." She gives him a motivational message for the day and asks him to identify exactly how he will use his time to accomplish his goals. She micromanages him and puts her energy into tracking down what he is doing. Tom and Tammy are in the overfunctioning/underfunctioning dance. This pattern never produces desired results for either person.

## Changing Patterns

You are the only one who can change these patterns for yourself. In your role as a team member, peer, or boss, it is healthy to consider these dynamics and where you may want to make changes in order to be more effective as a collaborator.

If you see that you want to change the dynamics in a relationship, it is also a signal that you are ready to grow to a new level of operating and a new level of collaboration. Let's explore the levels of business maturity and how they affect you.

## Levels of Maturity

Levels of maturity affect how we think about and craft conversations. They help us understand what we can and cannot hear in conversations. Understanding these levels of maturity enables us to reduce conflict and misunderstandings and continue to grow.

I first discovered this model in a course at the University of Pennsylvania. Janet Greco teaches the highly respected master's course called "Stories in Organizations: Tools for Executive Development." Taking that course was a powerful experience, as it enabled me to see group dynamics through the lens of maturity levels. One of the readings was a breakthrough trigger. In *Personal and Organizational Transformations: The True Challenge of Continual Quality Improvement* (The McGraw-Hill Developing Organizations Series), Fisher and Torbert (1995) propose a six-stage continuum of personal and professional development.

Their work inspired me, and since then I have built on their insights in my own work. I've researched how this model of development affects what we talk about and how we craft conversations with others, based on where we are now. I've added my own language, focused on the influence strategies of each level. Let me introduce you to this framework:

There are six stages of development or maturity that people have the potential to grow into. Each level is larger than the previous one, in that it includes all the possibilities from the former levels together with a new set of alternatives. At each stage we will be focused on different types of conversations. Our "That's for Me!" list will look very different at each of these stages of development.

## The Six Stages of Development

1. Getting my own needs met
2. Being liked by others
3. Being good at what I do
4. Getting broad results—having a big effect
5. Being principle focused
6. Being a life, business, or spiritual guru for others

Each stage is broader, deeper, and more complicated than the previous one. Most of us behave predominantly from one stage in our conversing, thinking, and acting.

I want to provide you with the awareness to identify the following:

- At what stage or level you currently operate
- At what level your peers, boss, and staff operate from most often
- Some ideas about how you can grow yourself and others to move into the next stage in development, if you want to do so

As we move from each stage, we take the conversation ability, thinking, behavior, and learning from that stage into the next one. When we are stressed, overwhelmed, or in fear, we tend to regress to lower levels. Let's explore the ways we communicate, think, and act that are typical in each of the six levels.

## Level 1: Getting My Needs Met

We are born into this level. Short-term thinking focused on getting current needs met fuels tactical, transactional communication and relationships. The person operating from this level is opportunistic; when needs aren't met in one relationship, he or she will quickly move toward someone who will meet those needs. Feedback, no matter where it comes from, is often ignored and never requested. Boasting about power, luck, and ability to break the rules is common. There is little self-control, self-regulation, or building for the future from this level. Demanding and threatening behavior is typical when one is angry or in control. "They are ALL my marbles. If you don't like it, leave" is implied in both actions and words. "An eye for an eye" may be the way of operating with others. Distrusting and blaming others are common at this level, as is using hostile humor or sexuality to get things done in a manipulative manner. The opportunistic mindset severely limits long-term collaborative relationships. Most relationships this person has are transactional. Some people do not mature beyond this level; however most move onto the next level early in life.

## What This Level Looks Like at Work

Ken was a director in the sales department of a market research firm. His staff called him "the bully." Others saw him as focused on the next step that would serve him and his projects. Ken did not take suggestions or feedback well, so his peers stopped trying to engage him in conversations to explore and share learning. People were afraid of Ken and believed that if you crossed him, he would have you fired. Ken also thought he was above the procedures, rules, and laws of the organization; if he could get away with it, then it was ethical in his opinion. He literally had a bullwhip on the table behind his desk. When he was talking to one of his team members, giving orders, he would play with the bullwhip in his hands as he spoke. Command and control guided Ken's conversations and actions.

## Level 2: Being Liked by Others

Being part of the group, well-liked, and able to get along are typical of this stage. Diplomatic, we tend to avoid taking risks and facing conflict at this level, learning the rules so we fit in. Socially expected behavior is prized. Ensuring that others know and follow the rules is important. There is a willingness to listen to positive feedback from those who are liked and part of the desired group. Knowing the social order or hierarchy is vital at this level, and telling others what they want to hear is common. Pleasing others may lead to placating conversations. Here we typically don't act as leaders of the group, but as followers, aspiring members of the group, or peers.

The desire to be heard and appreciated is a universal human need. We all experience this desire. This stage also has to do with how we heal the pain from not being heard and appreciated by people whose attention we want. What's learned at this stage is how to value ourselves enough so that our own opinion about what we are doing is more important than someone else's opinion, as well as learning how to balance this without reverting back to Level 1 (acting so arrogant that we don't hear others).

## What This Level Looks Like at Work

Bill was the team glue, because he provided loyalty and goodwill. "Be nice" was Bill's motto. Bill appeared to be unable to make decisions or recommendations on his own if conflict was apparent. Bill was risk-averse and would give in to whomever had a clear, strong point of view. He would not give performance feedback to others, because he worried it would hurt their feelings. Bill believed people were who they were and they were not going to change, so there was no reason to speak up and give guidance. He did everything he could to help others save face. It was comfortable working with him, unless there was conflict that needed to be resolved. As a result, no one grew around Bill—including Bill. Over time, Bill's peers felt annoyed with him, because he would not stand up to his management and instead accepted goal numbers that were way above what the team would be able to accomplish. Bill was a "company man" who never challenged anything, and therefore game-changing conversations did not occur in Bill's interactions with others. He was blind to other ways of engaging.

### Level 3: Being Good at What I Do

Mastery over a skill or technical ability is important here. The focus is on task efficiency over broad effectiveness. We are committed to high standards in the area of competency—being a technician or master, very focused on being perfect at our craft. At this stage we are quick to point out the faults or lack of competency in others and accept feedback only from those perceived to be better than we are at our particular skill. Our conversations are focused on competence, ability, skill level, and evaluation. We want to be considered unique and recognized for being the best. We worry that, if others have the same mastery of skills, we won't be considered unique or valued anymore, so we may not share information with those who want to learn. At this stage, we typically have high expectations of others and criticize others frequently, which may cause others to shut down in the relationship.

### What This Level Looks Like at Work

At his best, Jim was the go-to problem solver. He was unique in his software support department, because he was the only one who could solve the most complex problems for customers. Problem escalation ended at his office door. Jim was a perfectionist who would work late into the night to solve a problem. At his worst, Jim would not show the people in his department how he fixed the problem. He was openly critical of the way others did their jobs—including his boss. No one could live up to Jim's high standards. He hoarded projects and did not share his thinking with others to help them grow.

## Level 4: Getting Broad Results—
## Having a Big Effect

At this level we have long-term goals, see an inspiring future, welcome feedback from a wide variety of people, and value all accomplishments. Focused on achieving, we seek partnership with others instead of dominance, and we operate proactively, with a strategy to do what needs to be done. Working through differences of opinions and conflict to create resolutions is considered part of normal business. We accept a moral or values standard that may have been developed by others. Conversations focus on big-picture strategies that will lead to significant results. We feel personal emotional pain if we violate commitments or are disrespectful to others. At this level, people want to see the big picture and not get mired down in too much detail. They are willing to delegate and help others develop, and they are passionate about making an impact and leaving a lasting legacy.

### What This Level Looks Like at Work

Susan was hired into a role to build the recruiting function for a global, complex organization. When she was hired, she was asked to change the hiring practices companywide and to build a global team that would meet the future hiring needs of the organization. During her first year in the role, she had to deal with several cross-functional conflicts, because there was confusion about who owned the hiring processes within this huge organization. She collaborated with her bosses to create a strategy to resolve the long-term conflict that had existed before she joined the organization. Susan hired her own teams in London, Hong Kong, New York, and India. She was committed to creating a high-performing team reporting to her and to creating a culture of growth within her team. Susan led team development activities to ensure that each person knew his or her own role and how to work well with peers.

## Level 5: Being Principle Focused

By this level, judgment for making wise decisions has been honed. People who are principle-focused are effective strategists, with clear standards that have likely been self-developed, based on experience. Self-trust has evolved. These people are aware that their thoughts and feelings create outcomes, and they take responsibility for them. They understand complexity and paradox and enjoy variety, and even ambiguity. They see multiple sides of an issue. Conversations focus on being partners and collaborating for the common good and insuring that the principles of effectiveness will thrive. It is at this level that people begin to recognize, understand, and intentionally adapt to other people's needs, styles, and maturity levels. They no longer expect others to come to where they are in order for effective communication to occur. They have grown beyond the limitations of their preferred communication styles, have polished the edges of their own styles, and are now able to adapt communication to the needs of the conversation they are in.

## What This Level Looks Like at Work

Susan (whom we discussed in the previous example) was given an opportunity to work with a coach a few months into her new role, because the conflicts she was experiencing caused her to want a sounding board, someone who could help her grow and not get caught up in the details of the conflicts that existed in her organization. Susan also wanted to learn how to recognize, understand, and intentionally adapt to other people's needs, styles, and maturity levels. Because she was a quick learner, she mastered this skill in about six months and landed in this new level of maturity. As a result, in her second year in the role, she broadened her focus and began facilitating meetings with key leaders across the global organization to define future hiring needs as well as new strategies to meet the changing workforce demands. She built deep relationships with people that went beyond the specific role she was in—people talked with her about more than just her role's assignments—and she was heavily involved in designing the principles of leadership in the organization. Susan understood and enjoyed the ambiguity in her work. She tailored her communication to the specific needs of the person or group she was working with without having to work hard at doing so. Eventually, she was promoted to a higher level, which included having the Global Succession Planning Strategy team reporting into her as well.

## Level 6: Being a Life, Business, or Spiritual Guru for Others

At this level, people set the stage for others to win and succeed. They are more focused on transformation, seeking joy, lightness, order, and creation. They are highly disciplined. Others think what these "gurus" are doing seems magical, because amazing things keep happening. Both time and experiences are symbolic or metaphorical for people operating from this level in a way that may be hard for those not operating from this level to understand. Those who achieve Level 6 inspire growth by the way they are, the questions they ask, and the stories they share. Conversations are collaborative and often let the other person win, as there is no need to seek the spotlight.

### What This Level Looks Like at Work

The author of *What Got You Here Won't Get You There*, Marshall Goldsmith, appears to be living from Level 6. He is a business guru who coaches CEOs from Fortune 100 companies all over the world. He is a Buddhist who shares the Buddhist principles by role modeling them from the stage as well as in his coaching and his writing. Recently, Marshall was speaking to a very small group of people, and I was lucky enough to be sitting near him. He talked about the importance of getting unstuck. Buddhist wisdom for how to live life is sprinkled with one story after another; Goldsmith brings these ideas alive when he speaks. He ended his comments with this wise thought: "The person who has the power to make the decision makes the decision. Make peace with that." And with a deep belly laugh he was gone.

> *"Thousands of candles can be lighted from a single candle, and the life of a candle will not be shortened. Happiness never decreases by being shared."*
> —Buddha

When we understand these maturity stages and their role in our professional development, we can look at what is next for us. We have to master one level before we can move onto the next. In other words, we cannot leap over one level, hoping to mature faster. We can find someone who is already at the next stage, where we want to grow to, and begin to grow ourselves by watching and learning from his or her conversations. This whole book is designed to guide you to higher levels of business maturity, if that is what you choose.

The point of identifying your maturity level as well as the levels of the people you want to collaborate with is not to be right or to pigeonhole yourself or others, but rather to guide you to work more effectively together. There is one tricky thing to keep in mind, however. Unless we understand this framework, we do not tend to appreciate the thinking or conversation focus of people who are at two or more levels above or below where we are. For example, if I report to a manager who operates from Level 2, I will not likely be rewarded for operating from higher levels. A manager (or parent) at Level 3 will expect her staff members to be at that stage or lower. If you are communicating with someone who is operating from a level that is different from yours, consider how his maturity level will affect what is important to him and what he is focused on.

For this reason, as you grow you will want to find people who are also committed to growing with you—not enmeshed where you are now. Perhaps you will create a strategy for relationship building based on your current developmental level? Doing so will enable you to grow.

So far we've been exploring dynamics in one-to-one interactions. Now let's pull the camera lens back a bit and look at larger groups. When people come together, whether they have a goal yet or not, leadership roles will begin to emerge.

## Emergent Leadership Roles

There are four leader roles that begin to evolve early in a group's meeting. Within 12 hours of the group members interacting, these roles will be established. Usually, these emerge in the order shown below:

1. **Task leader:** This person sets the agenda, assigns tasks and roles, and allocates resources. On a healthy team, this person participates, engages others, and is open to communicating and listening. On an unhealthy team, this person is a dictator or tyrant.
2. **Emotion or morale leader:** This person watches for the morale of the group, gets to know people as individuals, and encourages people to share their thoughts and feelings. On a healthy team, this person is a trusted colleague who is a sounding board for uncovering ideas and feelings, so that one does not get stuck. On an unhealthy team, this person gossips, pits people against each other, and creates tension in the team.
3. **Fun leader or scapegoat:** This person, on a healthy team, lightens the intensity, encourages playful interactions, ensures that team members take breaks and laugh. On an unhealthy team, this person is blamed or criticized; he or she becomes the scapegoat for people not taking responsibility for their own actions.

4. **Challenger leader:** This person challenges the task leader's thinking, agenda, process, and goals. On a healthy team, this person speaks up directly to the task leader and works out the blind spots in the task leader's style and thinking. On an unhealthy team, this person goes underground, sabotaging the task leader's role and power.

When a person in one of these emergent leadership roles moves off the team, another person moves into the emergent leadership role. In other words, sometimes a new manager will get rid of the challenger leader, not realizing that someone else will assume that role. It is wise for the task leader to align with and make good use of the feedback that comes from the challenger leader and the other types of leaders on the team. How do you do that? I'm going to show you how to do this.

When I lead workshops on team building and development, I discuss these roles and ask participants to identify the people playing these leadership roles on their past teams. Participants immediately get it and see the emergent leadership roles in their own experience.

The leadership role you prefer to play is likely to be one you have played on many teams or within family groups. Sometimes we find ourselves in a team dynamic where we are in a role we do not like. Maybe you do not enjoy being the challenger leader, but you find yourself in that role with a new boss who just took over the department. You are the most senior person on the team, so the group defers to you to challenge the new thinking. A conflict can emerge internally when the role one is cast into does not align with one's preferred communication style.

Now that you are aware of these four emergent leader roles, you can begin to think about which one or ones you want to play as you collaborate to get results at work.

After group leaders emerge, the individuals may decide they want to become a team. When that happens, there are predictable stages of team development that affect group dynamics.

## Stages of Team Development

Dr. Bruce Wayne Tuckman is an American psychologist who researched the theory of group dynamics. He is currently a professor of educational psychology at Ohio State University. Dr. Tuckman created a useful model for understanding the predictable stages of team development. What we approach in collaborating will be different in each of these stages.

1. Forming
2. Storming
3. Norming
4. Performing
5. Adjourning

His research revealed that groups return to the Forming stage whenever there is a change in the group's goals or team members. Many groups get stuck in one stage; only 29 percent of teams ever reach the performing stage. Reaching stage 4 and being a high-performing group requires regular attention to team maintenance as well as task functions.

I've built on this model, and I use it with coaching clients to help them navigate building teams as well as serving as a team member when collaborating with peers. Here is what you need to know to be effective collaborating during each stage:

### Stage 1. Forming

New team members commonly experience these feelings:

Excitement and optimism about being part of the team

Pride at being selected for the team

Tentativeness about attachment to this new group—will they accept me?

Anxiety about the tasks ahead and fear of failure—will the people on the team have the skills to do what needs to be done?

Actions the team leader needs to take during the forming stage include:

Help people get to know each other.

Identify and prioritize the goals and vision for the group.

Inquire about team members' hopes, fears, and expectations.

Establish ground rules for independent action, participation, resolving conflict, presenting ideas, and reaching consensus.

Identify the roles and responsibilities of the team members and ensure that they understand them.

Hold meetings focused on having the team members share their preferred communication styles and workplace motivators, and how they like to add value to the team.

Make decisions and do not expect the team members to be able to make decisions together on their own yet.

## Stage 2. Storming

During the storming stage, team members commonly experience these feelings:

Frustration at the lack of progress

Anxiety over miscommunication and problems with teamwork

Fear of different communication styles and different people

Fluctuations between optimism and pessimism about the group's chances of succeeding

It is common to see these types of behaviors when a team is in the storming stage:

Questioning the purpose, goals, tasks, and processes

Arguing among team members

Staking out areas of expertise

Forming subgroups

Complaining about the workload

Resisting leadership and influence from others

Actions the team leader needs to take during the storming stage include:

Bring underlying issues to the surface and encourage the expression of feelings and possible solutions to the issues.

Define the roles and accountabilities of the team members and play to each team member's strengths.

Create subgroups to make decisions, but mix subgroup members; focus on major issues with the entire group together.

Model listening skills to every member of the team, not just favorite members.

Be solution focused; ask questions that focus on what the team leader wants to create.

Make decisions and move through conflict; don't keep conflicts alive for long periods of time.

Do not ignore the conflicts; that will cause them to get bigger.

## Stage 3. Norming

During the norming stage, team members commonly experience these feelings:

Relief that the tension and conflict have subsided

Renewed confidence in the team's abilities

Increased willingness to be seen as a team member

Willingness to give and receive developmental feedback; more openness to listening

Increased caring for members of the team

It is common to see these types of behaviors when a team is in the norming stage:

Enforcing of group norms and standards

Communicating more openly and directly

Cooperating with a focus on group goals

Negotiating, rather than competing, for resources

Testing for and building group consensus

Sharing feelings and personal issues and being more authentic with each other

Giving overt attention to the team's maintenance needs and functions

Actions the team leader needs to take during the norming stage include:

Speak the hidden norms and help the team to evaluate and set new norms.

Help the team to develop a unique identity.

Challenge the team members' boundaries individually.

Coach the team members in building new skills and sharing what they know.

Use consensus building and explore areas of difference.

Invite input and feedback on every major decision.

Let the team members make some decisions on their own together.

## Stage 4. Performing

During the performing stage, team members commonly experience these feelings:

Acceptance of each others' strengths and developmental areas

Trust in the others and willingness to be vulnerable

Comfort in dealing with differences and resolving conflict

Pride in being part of the team

It is common to see these types of behaviors when a team is in the performing stage:

Adapting personal styles to the needs of the project

Multilateral influencing within the group

Openly communicating thoughts and feelings

Encouraging everyone to use his or her voice and be heard by the team

Managing and resolving conflict and encouraging and discussing differences

Enjoying collaborating

Giving and receiving coaching feedback at the deepest levels because trust is so high

Identifying strongly with the team and having deep pride in the accomplishments of the team

Actions the team leader needs to take during the performing stage include:

Sit back and enjoy! Let them lead!

Use consensus for all major team decisions.

Give lots of positive feedback.

Experiment and explore process improvements.

Encourage the group to develop evaluation criteria; do not do the work for the team.

Celebrate and affirm accomplishments.

Arrange ceremonies for closure and for assimilating new members into the group.

### Stage 5. Adjourning

During the adjourning stage, team members commonly experience these feelings:

Apprehension over loss of group identity

Pride in the group's achievements

Reluctance to let go

Regret over any poorly managed conflicts or endings

It is common to see these types of behaviors when a team is in the adjourning stage:

Evaluating results and producing final status reports

Being willing or unwilling to let go

Wanting recognition and appreciation

Saying good-bye and having conversations for closing

Actions the team leader needs to take during the adjourning stage include:

Establish closing procedures for the team.

Discuss endings with team members individually and as a group.

Provide a way for team members to acknowledge what they appreciate about each other.

End with a ritual that honors the group and each of its members.

Group dynamics emerge any time people work together. When you are aware of the different dynamics at play, you can be a more effective collaborator. Effective collaboration is a positive group dynamic in which we achieve desired results. When members of a team are overly fixated on each other, they lose sight of the common goals and become ineffective. In partnerships, decisions are made jointly and the decision-making process is agreed upon by all parties involved. In enmeshed relationships one person often takes control of the other, which can create a one-up-one-down dynamic and under- and overperformers.

We are constantly evolving and changing. Therefore, our group dynamics and collaborations will also change. We can progress from focusing on our own needs to a level of maturity in which we focus on meeting the needs of others, who are professionally developing themselves. The key to progress through the developmental stages is to ask yourself this question after difficult situations, "What would need to exist for me to look back on this and be glad it happened, because it helped me grow?" This attitude will keep you moving forward towards being a more mature person and a more effective collaborator.

## Kristy Tan Neckowicz's Story: Schedule Chicken

Kristy Tan Neckowicz, PMP, former vice president of Oracle's Primavera Global Business Unit, gave a presentation at the Project Management Institute titled, "Winning the Game of Schedule Chicken." Her presentation provided an "aha!" moment for people about reading group dynamics and collaborating across departments or divisions as it relates to how schedules are managed. I appreciated what Kristy shared about what can and does happen in organizations, especially where there are complex schedules that are being managed across several groups. Her insights are useful to become a savvy collaborator who can solve group dysfunction.

Kristy started her presentation by asking, "Have you ever played the game called 'Chicken'?" Two or more players are required. The objective is to be the last player to quit whatever the action is that you have agreed to do. The loser is labeled "chicken" and the winner gets bragging rights. Perhaps you've seen games of Chicken in movies like *Top Gun* and *Rebel without a Cause.*

In "Schedule Chicken," two or more teams compete to see who will be the first to admit that schedule milestones cannot be met. The loser team is chastised and someone will have to pay for the faults as a scapegoat. When that happens, all the other teams will be able to breathe a sigh of relief, but the entire project will suffer schedule delays.

This is the typical strategy for playing the game:

Commit to an unrealistic milestone date.

Ensure that the due date is even more unrealistic for another team.

Keep schedule slippage a secret until it is absolutely apparent.

Shine the light on other teams, who are also running late.

Never be the first to say that you can't keep the schedule.

Why do people in organizations play a game like this? Dysfunction. People do it in all areas of business often because leaders are rewarding the wrong things and creating internal competition, not collaboration.

Although it may be human nature to engage in this kind of negative competitive behavior, that doesn't mean the behavior can't be changed. It can! Knowing it can occur is the first step; understanding the circumstances that precipitate it is the second step in changing the dysfunctional dynamic.

Why do project teams continue to play this game? Here are some reasons:

**Job security:** Make it less likely for management intervention.

**Fear:** Don't shoot the messenger.

**Breathing room:** Delay the recovery effort and rework.

**Wishful thinking:** More resources will become available later; schedule delays can be absorbed into later phases; another area of the project will overrun; there will be more time later to resolve issues.

**Lack of long-term commitment to the organization:** I may not be here when this blows up, so why make it happen now while I am here?

The true and long-term damage of a culture that encourages and allows schedule chicken is a disaster that keeps repeating. According to Peter Schuh, author of *Integrating Agile Development in the Real World*: "For project management, Schedule Chicken is an iterative game, where the most dishonest and deceptive participant wins and is encouraged to hone his destructive behavior so as to win again in the next round. In management environments that foster schedule chicken, transparency and honesty are inadvertently discouraged and even punished." This game causes bigger problems for the organization; it is also a signal that there are larger leadership problems playing out organizationally.

If Schedule Chicken is occurring in your organization, you may see this pattern occurring:

1. Project schedule appears to be exactly on track.
2. Project schedule suddenly experiences a massive schedule delay.
3. Someone (or a team) is labeled as the culprit.
4. Project deadlines are officially extended.

Steps 1–4 repeat.
This game includes the following cast of characters:

*The Novice Chicken:* a relatively new member or unwilling accomplice who is clueless about the game and may inadvertently expose his or her team.

*Chicken Little:* the team member with a "the-sky-is-falling" reputation, who speculates and exposes delays; no one takes him or her seriously anymore.

*The Yellow Bird:* an eternal optimist who is liked by most players, who soothes and calms the chicken littles, and cautions or quiets the novice chickens before embarrassment occurs.

*The Hawk:* the bully who believes in survival of the fittest is never the first to confess there is a problem and never accepts blame.

*The Love Bird:* the harmonizer identifies the types of players, tries to create alignment, wants to negotiate resolutions, and anticipates players changing their natures.

No one wins schedule chicken in the long term; even when it looks like there are short-term winners, the losses add up over time.

Want to stop this pattern in your organization? A little education goes a long way. Make sure every team rewards these behaviors:

Understanding the project's goals

Placing successes of the project above the team or member

Agreeing on realistic target dates, given the capacity upfront

Knowing the dangers of multi-tasking

Providing tools for tracking progress against plan

Teaching techniques of variance analysis and forecasting

How do you do that? Use the following basic critical path concepts:

Identify the "critical chain"—the longest chain of tasks through the project, considering all the resource limitations.

Ensure the task durations are aggressive and not padded.

Focus on the task at hand; avoid multi-tasking.

Add "buffers" in strategic places to protect the project end dates.

Manage the buffers as a team; collaborate across the organization with all information available.

To stop the game of schedule chicken in your organization, build real trust and relationships among team members. Authentically collaborate by:

Knowing the culture and the desired state

Establishing and enforcing ground rules

Designing reward systems for the desired behaviors

Creating open and safe forums for full disclosure

Nurturing an environment of trust and transparency

The real winners in business are those that have rid their organizations of games like schedule chicken and instead cultivate leaders who can distinguish the dynamics among people. The outstanding leaders that succeed, time after time, are the ones that build partnerships within their organizations and foster higher levels of trust, maturity, and collaboration. They develop teams focused on the interactions between team members, so that the game of schedule chicken is not rewarded.

## Group Dynamics Application Exercise

Where do you experience partnership and where do you experience enmeshment?

Think about a key relationship in your life, perhaps with your boss, a peer, your spouse, or maybe even your mother. Are you partners or are you enmeshed in each other? Use this new lens to look at several relationships you have. What do you notice? What action do you want to take as a result of this awareness?

Explore your relationships and how decisions are made; are you acting as partners? Discuss how a decision will be made and ask clearly for what you want. Do you have a relationship in which you need to shift from being in the one-up-one-down pattern? Use Spencer Johnson's "Yes" or "No" guide to decision-making questions, described earlier in this chapter, the next time you are faced with a complex decision and you want to collaborate with others to make the decision.

Are there any overfunctioning or underfunctioning patterns you want to change in relationships you have at work? How could you use what you have learned here to begin to make this change?

What would need to exist for you to move to the next level of maturity? Look at your list of team members and colleagues. Identify someone who often operates from the next level. Begin to create opportunities to talk regularly with that person, so you can examine his or her forward movement. What actions can you take to continue your own professional development toward a higher level of maturity?

What stage of team development is your current team operating from? How can you use this information to guide the right discussions for collaborating with your team as a peer or leader?

Reflection question: What maturity level would someone be coming from if he regularly plays schedule chicken? Consider the level of maturity and the framework for group dynamics someone would have if he rewards schedule chicken. High-performing teams and organizations have grown beyond playing schedule chicken. If you are a leader in your organization, you have the ability to stop rewarding schedule-chicken games. If you are a team member and schedule chicken is being played, create a partnership conversation with your team leader and discuss what you see happening.

# CHAPTER 8

# Storytelling

All of us create narratives about who we are and where we are going. The stories we tell about ourselves make a huge difference in how others see us and how we create our futures. Storytelling is a skill that we need to develop to be effective communicators who can inspire others to see the vision of where we are coming from and going together.

Let's explore what story you and your organization may be telling. To do so, I'll introduce you to an archetypal model about how we cast ourselves into roles and plot lines. Storytelling is so ingrained in how we think that we may not even be aware of these plot lines as we use them. The story or context we put around what we are doing will often fit into one of these nine plot lines:

> **The victim:** "I almost got what I wanted, but then this horrible thing happened. This is awful. I have no power, no ability to make my own choices." This role also includes stories of passively waiting for someone else to notice what we are capable of doing—"I'm still waiting for a mentor to tap me on the shoulder, to notice that I am capable of being a star performer. Why don't I have a mentor guiding me?"

**The blame game:** "It is his fault I am here. Someone else has done me wrong. My boss is horrible at coaching team members, and it's all his fault that we don't work well together." "Suzy is impossible to get along with—if she were not on the team, we could get more done. No one notices all the capabilities and competencies I have to offer, and because of that, nothing good is happening to me yet."

**The loss/sad tale:** Loss of a job, dream, loved one. "I'm stuck, because I lost what was most important to me."

**The revenge story:** "Because I was hurt by someone, I am now going to be miserable to get him back, or I am going to find a way to hurt him too. Because I don't get along with my team member Joe, I don't want to do something nice for him."

**The stranger in a strange land:** "I'm not in Kansas anymore. I'm going to watch what is going on here and figure out how to respond." Elements of change and a new adventure or path are evidence of this plot line. Seeing new possibilities and being an explorer or seeker may emerge here.

**The quest adventure:** "I've just been promoted, and I am going to learn how to lead." "My boss just told me he is going to retire in six months. I want to demonstrate I am ready for his job when he retires." This story is about seeking, striving to get somewhere, traveling on a new path.

**The rags-to-riches triumph:** "I was there, and now I am here. Look how far I've come!" This story line often has an inspiring message that goes something like, "If I can do it, you can too! You can turn your situation around and be a success."

**The hero or problem-solver story:** "There was a problem, and my team worked together to find a solution—we made great things happen. We were in a complex situation and created extraordinary results!" Despite the odds, because of personal integrity and hard work, success was achieved.

**The passion or love story:** "I love my job! This is the best organization I've ever worked with." This could be a story about two people, or it could be about how much someone loves his life, his team, or his company. It could be appreciating being kindred spirits with a colleague or team one is working with.

Our communication with ourselves and others is filled with these story plot lines. These form the context around which our actions evolve. Begin to notice the most common plot lines in your thinking. Notice which plot line you were operating from before you began reading this book today. Can you think of people who are run by sad stories or passion stories? Have you noticed that every time they show up they share examples of why they deserve to be sad or passionate? Can you think of someone you interact with frequently who is grounded in the hero-story plot line?

Which story you hang out in is your choice.

The story we tell affects other people's motivation to collaborate with us. Each of these stories has an emotional wake that comes with it. If we are telling victim stories, we are spreading that sentiment to ourselves and then to others. It extends outward like ripples. If we are telling blame-game stories, we are likely triggering anger in ourselves, and maybe in others too. When we tell loss stories, we are triggering sadness. When we tell revenge stories, we feel envy. Stranger-in-a-strange-land stories may trigger fear and then hope. The quest and rags-to-riches stories are about hope and excitement. The love or passion story triggers the highest level of feelings—joy and love. What emotions are you triggering as a result of the plot line you share most often? You will be known by the emotional wake you create as a result of the story line you repeat.

Hope, love, and joy inspire collaboration. Do others perceive you as someone who inspires collaboration and creates a shared vision?

## Spot the Plot

All of us have habitual ways of thinking. Over and over, we retell these plots, often unaware we are doing so. Begin to spot the plot you are using in your communication with the people you want to collaborate with. Are you inspiring people to achieve new results?

The good news is that you can change your habitual story if you desire to.

Many years ago, I experienced several profoundly sad experiences back-to-back, including the death of two people who were very close to me. Knowing this, many people who worked with me began to walk on eggshells around me. Before very long, I realized that I was living a sad-story plot line and others were responding to me accordingly. I had a private conversation with myself and decided I did not want that loss to be the story of my life. I wanted a larger life for myself, and I was willing to step out of the loss story to intentionally create something better for myself and others. Would you like to do the same thing?

A rags-to-riches story plot line just occurred—did you catch it? These story plot lines can occur in a sentence or two.

When we do not have a compelling story that creates meaning, purpose, and focus for our lives, we feel lost and rudderless. Someone else's agenda may be leading the way.

If you want to change a plot line that has held you back, it will be important to catch yourself in that plot line and stop telling that story. You can change the story of your career and life if you want to. That is what career transitions are about.

## Jenny's Story

Jenny showed up to a volunteer activity that I lead, looking forward to meeting the other volunteers and making new friends. Her friendly facial expression and happy tone of voice brought people to her as they waited in the lobby.

This group of people did not know each other, and yet they realized they would be working closely together as volunteers on a project for three months. After brief introductions, the first assignments were given out to smaller teams. I encouraged team members to introduce themselves in their smaller groups and talk with each other while beginning the first work assignment. When Jenny introduced herself, she talked about how challenging her regular job was and how relieved she was to have a break, because she struggled in her relationship with her boss, who was not acting on her ideas. Jenny's frustration with her boss was obvious. The next day, during another activity, Jenny initiated some small talk by asking if anyone had heard about the problems that had occurred following the local school's prom. She shared details of students creating post-prom trouble and highlighted a supposed incident in which three teenage boys assaulted a young girl. Jenny appeared very interested in this local news, but another group member changed the subject quickly. Jenny's facial expression said she wasn't sure why the topic was changed so abruptly, but she went with the flow and did not bring it up again.

The next day while the team was walking together to a new building, Jenny asked if any of the group members were familiar with the challenges that occurred in a past historic event. Jenny described horrific acts against people that had occurred 20 years earlier. No one responded to Jenny's sharing. At this point, as the leader of this group, I felt the need to intervene to guide Jenny's sharing. Later I said to her privately: "Jenny, we are just getting to know each other, but I am noticing a pattern to the stories you are telling; they have been about helpless victims. Others on the team do not seem to be engaged when you share this type of story, and it's diverting the energy in the team. Some people seem to shy away from you when you tell this type of story. I'm not asking you to tell me, but I wonder if you are aware that your focus on victim stories is having an impact on the team."

She looked at me with a shocked expression. Perhaps most people would not say this to her. Since we would be working closely together for the next three months, I wanted to build a relationship that would work for both of us. This conversation was a game-changing moment. Jenny said, "I've never thought about that." I replied: "When you introduced yourself to the group, you talked about how difficult your boss is and how much you struggle in your job because he does not listen to you. Then later you brought up news examples of people who are victims. I have not heard you tell any other type of story since I met you. I wanted to bring it to your attention, since I would like all of us to work well as a team. We can achieve this by engaging with each other in an inspiring way, not from a victim mindset. Well-crafted stories can transform hopeless situations into problem-solving adventures. They can evoke the best in human nature to come together and cocreate what one person could not do alone. Victim stories can bring team members down, so they are not inspired to take on the challenges they will face. What do we want to do together?"

A few days later Jenny pulled me aside and said: "Thank you so much for saying that to me. I had never realized I was pro-jecting myself as a victim. I asked several of my friends about this, and they said I have been doing this with them for a long time. I am stunned that no one ever pointed this out to me before. At first it stung when you said it. I suspect that was because I knew it was true and I did not like that. Thank you so much for saying something to me. I am working on being aware when I am thinking like a victim, so I can change the way I project myself. I want to be a member of a team that is inspired and creates positive results, and I'm learning that, to do so, I have to change my story first."

Jenny and I trusted each other from then on. Vulnerability has a way of doing that. When one person is vulnerable with another and it is handled well, a deeper level of trust emerges. Our project was full of exciting hurdles that we worked through together. The foundation of trust that was established by this conversation made a big difference in how we worked together. To this day, we remain professional friends.

## Collin's Story

Collin is a vice president in a public relations department. He shared the following account with me:

> I've been thinking about the two principles we discussed in our last coaching conversation and how they fit together. The first one is believing that I am responsible, versus blaming others, when things do not go the way I wanted them to. The second is being solutions-focused instead of focused on problems (complaining). These two principles have created a fundamental shift in my thinking and the story I am telling, which in turn is altering how I interact with other people and approach challenges of all sizes.
>
> Here are two examples from today in which I handled things differently than I would have in the past:
>
> We have a shortage of parking spots, and we have some construction going on now to address the problem. In the short term, the construction makes the problem worse. When I came back to the office from an off-site meeting, there were no spots left. I ended up looking for a parking spot for 15 minutes and had to walk several blocks to get to the office after parking in an expensive garage. I caught myself having a frustrated "victim" story in my thinking and rationalizing why I was late for a meeting as a result. I

stopped. I was able to tell myself to knock it off, to see my own responsibility, and get focused back on what is worthwhile, what I want to create. I do not enjoy complaining anymore, so I stopped. When I arrived, I apologized for being late to the meeting and jumped into the agenda, rather than dramatically explaining what happened and bringing everyone else into my frustration.

Feeling good about my ability to self-regulate my story, I arrived back at my office, and Emma, one of my direct reports, told me what she was dealing with. She was very angry about an exchange she had with a customer-service supervisor. It seems the customer-service person demanded that Emma update a portion of our company intranet with some important updates. Emma had never been told this was expected of her nor had she been trained to do it. Emma thought that it was the job of customer service to update the intranet. The customer-service person shared her upset viewpoint in an e-mail about Emma not performing her duties and copied many people, pointing a finger negatively at Emma. In our conversation, I was able to guide Emma to pick up the phone and call the customer-service supervisor and ask for what she wanted. Emma said, "I was unaware this was expected of me. No one has ever mentioned this previously. . . . Going forward, if there is something that you expect me to do, I request that you discuss it directly with me rather than copy others who are not involved on an e-mail. Are you willing to pick up the phone and talk it out if there is an issue in the future?" The customer-service supervisor then apologized to Emma. I guided Emma to focus on the best way to get the updates done in the future. With my increased awareness, it is much easier to see how unproductive complaining about the situation is, especially compared to an approach that puts everyone's concerns out in the open, and then focused on preventing a recurrence in the future.

Because Collin is catching himself in the story he is telling and shifting to a more productive one, he is also becoming more aware of how to help his team members to do the same.

## Paul's Story

Paul seemed unclear about what he really wanted. Paul realized he had been operating from his domineering boss's agenda for the past several years of his career. He was in a victim-story plot line. Paul said, "I no longer seem to know what I want for myself as a result. I'm not motivated, and feel as if I am in a rat race." So I asked him, "Paul, what do you want to feel?" He looked at me with an annoyed expression, but I persisted, "Paul, I want you to describe for me what you want to feel. Describe what you would like to be saying to me a year from now." Paul began to imagine this. He said he wanted to feel "jubilant from the success" he created with his new team. Then I asked him, "Paul, what happened just before you felt this jubilant success?" He described his team members meeting to debrief the results of working with a new million-dollar client, discussing what was working for this client, and reading a letter the client had written to him about how much they were adding value. The contract would be renewed for another year. I took notes on what Paul was saying. Then I asked again, "What happened just before that?" After asking this question over and over until we were back to the moment when he first began to speak about his desire to feel "jubilant," we had the sequence of what he really wanted to do. We created it backwards, based on what he wanted to feel. The desired feeling is what motivates us. Paul now had a plan of action that could keep him inspired and on an adventure. This approach may work for you too, if you can imagine the end results but cannot envision how to get there.

Next I asked Paul to imagine taking each step that he had identified forward from today. As we did this, I asked: "Is there anything you would add here at this step? Anything else you need to consider? Is there anyone you would want to involve at this point?" We filled in the gaps. Going forward through this sequence turned it into a clear action plan for Paul, with each completed step becoming an item for his "That's for Me!" list.

After we finished the process of fleshing out Paul's action plan, I asked him to create a story about how he came to have this plan and why it was so important, so inspiring, to him. For all of us the key turning points—the places where we make transitions—tend to be much more obvious in the retelling of them than they are when we live them. Looking for the common threads—the values and motivators that tie our decisions and experiences together—is a worthwhile activity. Renowned sociolinguist Charlotte Linde works at the NASA Ames Research Center as a research scientist. Linde has studied the importance of coherence in our life stories. She says that continuity and causality are vital to creating coherence in our stories. In other words, we must explain who we are—what our character is, share both personal and professional reasons for creating change, and reframe our past in light of the changes we are now seeking. Stories enable us to reinvent ourselves and our organizations, based on where we want to go.

Central to your work as a business leader or inspiring collaborator is crafting a story that engages people. The power of storytelling—the ability to share your story or your company's story—is crucial in every phase of business. A great salesperson knows how to inspire a customer with a story about how this product or service will enable the customer to be a hero. The manager who successfully rallies the team to envision extraordinary results and then stick with the plan to build those outcomes is the one who is tapped on the shoulder for the next promotion. The CEO who brings the company's mission alive with an emotional connection is the one who secures financing, partners, and star performers to join the adventure.

## Storytelling Application Exercise

With regard to the nine different story plot lines, whom do you know who is known for telling each of these stories?

Which of these stories inspire you? Which ones do you prefer to hang out in?

Which story plot lines do you want to be known for? What do you want the story of your professional life to be? What else do you want to be known for? When you think about your own career story of how you got here, what is it that makes your story coherent? Is there a passion or theme you have developed that ties your transitions together? Create a clear story about this for yourself and begin to share it with others. Doing so creates your professional brand.

# CHAPTER 9

# When Conflict Stops Progress: Creating More Effective Conversations That Lead to Resolution

## What Causes Conflicts?

Sometimes when conflicts arise it is not because either person is being purposefully aggressive or confrontational. Differing communication styles and motivators can cause conflicts. How can you tell if a conflict is about values or communication style? When a conflict is based on *how* something is being done, on behaviors, then it is rooted in communication style. When a conflict is about beliefs of what is right or wrong, valuable or having no value, then it is based on values and underlying motivators. (I use the words *values* and *motivators* to mean the same thing because what we value is what motivates us.)

The most challenging conflicts are the ones that are based on differences in motivators. When conflict arises from differing beliefs about what is right or wrong, good or bad, worthy or unworthy, then it becomes more difficult to create shared purpose and goals. Reasoning, negotiation, and problem solving are unlikely to have positive results when the conflict results from a clash of values.

When people are angry because they feel like they have not been heard, they need to find a way to voice their concerns, so the person whose attention they want can hear them. This is likely when different communication styles and motivators are being expressed.

### How Each Communication Style Addresses Conflict

People who prefer the Dominant Communication Style address conflict directly; they may even appear to those preferring other styles to enjoy starting conflict. They are known for tackling issues head-on, so that they may seem belligerent and argumentative to others. They do not see themselves this way and may find it surprising to learn that others struggle in relating to their direct confrontational style. It is not uncommon for them to interrupt others and increase the volume and intensity of their voices. Others may think they yell or get too intense, but people with a Dominant style often do not realize this. They value honesty, and they dislike anything that looks like beating around the bush or being too diplomatic. With this style it is best to match the person's intensity, be direct and candid, and ask clearly for what you need in order to move forward. Stick to facts and focus on desired results and actions. Be prepared to make quick decisions. The High Dominant style communicator loves to make decisions and would be willing to revisit a decision again in a few days or weeks.

People who prefer the Influence Communication Style address conflict directly, based on what they are feeling. They do not hesitate to describe their feelings about issues and those with other styles may think they go on and on, becoming overly dramatic or exaggerating the intensity of an experience. Others may be overwhelmed or feel manipulated by this person's emotions during a conversation for conflict resolution. With those using this style it is best to help them by creating a pros-and-cons list for every proposed solution. Be prepared to talk out each part and ask questions to help them think beyond the initial feelings they have about the issue. Influencers need to verbalize an idea to be clear about what they are thinking. Help them to look at potential unintended consequences of solutions and avoid letting their persuasive abilities drown your thinking. Do not let them push you into agreeing through an emotional appeal, if you have not had time to consider a desired outcome for yourself.

People who prefer the Steady Communication Style are unlikely to reveal their own feelings and opinions about the issue. They often appear passive to others. They may avoid conflict at all costs. They appear to give in or placate to avoid a fight or public disagreement. This often leads people with different communication styles to see them as being weak and perhaps even dishonest, because they seem unwilling to address the real issues. With people employing this style it is best to emphasize your desire to continue a strong relationship. State that a successful resolution to this issue will be achieved more quickly by focusing on the issue objectively. Be patient and allow time for the Steady communicator to work through her cautious thinking and feelings. Do not push for quick decisions in meetings. Provide two or three days to sleep on the issue, and allow for thinking to evolve. These people prefer to make a decision once and stick with it for a very long time.

People who prefer the Compliant-to-Standards Communication Style address conflict by becoming entrenched in their facts, data, and research when a conflict emerges. They are often uncomfortable with other people's emotions and do not know how to process themselves or others through emotions by deep listening. It is as if they wear blinders to emotions. Others perceive them as tight, insensitive, rigid, and unwilling to compromise during conflict-resolution discussions. With people employing this communication style it is best to avoid becoming emotional or impatient with their inability to deal with emotions. Focus on facts and logic with them—not emotions. Do not insist on having your feelings recognized or try to seek validation of your feelings. Give him time to process and think through the situation alone. Two or three days later, the person using a Compliant style may circle back to you and say that he has given the issue much thought and has an option for a resolution.

## Tamara's Story (Continued from Chapter 2)

Although Tamara has been working at her job for five years, she wanted different results at work. She was ready to get out of a rut she had been in for too long. Tamara felt her boss was not hearing her. Over time she had developed a "no-one-hears-me" victim thought pattern that came through loudly when she was working with her team. To change this, first Tamara admitted to herself that she was ready to make some big changes, so that she could create a community of positive collaboration around her. Tamara had to admit she was not accomplishing what she wanted. She saw she was in a conflict with herself about what to do. Then she needed to look at the style differences between her and her boss.

Tamara's preferred communication style is High Compliant-to-Standards with a Steady style as backup. Tamara has a Low Dominant communication drive. She had been expecting other people, including her boss, to use her style when speaking to her. Tamara was not flexing or adapting her communication to others' needs. When Tamara and I began to talk about communication style patterns, Tamara was able to see immediately that her boss's pattern was the opposite of hers. Tamara's boss prefers a High Influence Communication Style with a Dominant backup. They are directly across the communication style wheel from each other. As you already know from the chapter on communication styles, we have the most difficulty understanding communication from people who are opposite us on the Success Insights Wheel. Our communication patterns are very different. How we handle conflict is very different when we are opposite each other on the communication style wheel.

Tamara had been taking it personally when her boss did not respond as she thought he should. She assumed a negative intent from him, based on their style differences. To work through the conflict common with this communication style difference,

Tamara had to overcome her own bitterness and stuck-in-a-rut thought pattern. She had to stop assuming she already knew her boss's intentions. She needed to understand his perspective. She began to think about how he needed information. Because he has a High Influence style with a Dominant backup, he likes a fast pace and wants the big picture first, with a clear request instead of lots of details building up to a request after several conversations. He wants to make decisions quickly and is open to changing his mind frequently; he likes to know who is aligned with whom and wants more friendly interaction. He even appreciates an emotional appeal for action, because he wants to be inspired. Instead, Tamara had been very tight-lipped, aloof, and distant with him. She had presented facts, data, and logic, intending to build a case over time, leading him to see all the research she had done and how that led her to certain conclusions. Tamara had to admit to herself that she was creating tension in their communication, because he does not think like this. He saw her as being in the weeds, too analytical, and much too distant for him to align with. The underlying conflict between them was as much on her shoulders as it was on his, but because she was the one with the awareness, it was on her to take the actions to resolve the conflicts between them.

Since Tamara wants a change in their relationship, she is the one who needs to adapt to his preferred communication style. She prefers a Compliant Steady style, but her boss prefers an Influence Dominant style. He wants a fast-paced, fun-friendly environment, so she now begins conversations by asking questions with a more upbeat, friendly tone of voice than she would otherwise use. She may ask after a long weekend, "How are you doing? What fun have you been brewing?" She knows he loves to make decisions quickly and will be willing to change his mind much more frequently than she would be, so she asks, "What decisions would you like to make in our meeting today?" When in a meeting, she asks, "What is your gut telling you?" and she is open to engage on a more emotional level with him than she was previously. Tamara intentionally uses more direct eye contact and a facial expression that says she is interested in what he has to say. She doubles her pace and deletes the long pauses when speaking with him. She initiates conversations more frequently, asking, "What is on your mind?" She realizes he will appreciate more verbal recognition than she was giving previously. She now looks for things to acknowledge, "You did a great job on the opening of the team meeting. I liked the way you asked everyone to share their favorite movie and why they liked it before we dove into the numbers today."

When Tamara began to do this, she experienced a resolution to their conflict and better results. You can experience the same positive results by learning how to blend your communication style with someone else's, as Tamara did. Following is a specific guide on how to blend your style for each of the style patterns that emerge.

## Blending Your Style

You already know that all people are not alike. To communicate successfully with others, you will need to learn how to blend your own preferred communication style with that of the person you are presenting to. Each style requires a different approach, and will respond to you in different ways. By "blending" your style with theirs, your conversations and presentations will achieve maximum success. In order to do this, you compare the strong and weak points of your own style with those of your different audience members and adjust yours accordingly. Following is information you need to prepare for each style.

### Basic Patterns and Approaches

Learn to interpret patterns and the most common acts that go along with them. This will enable you to establish rapport that enables people to feel at ease with you. After the initial period of relationship building, you can relax and make minor adjust-

**TABLE 9.1** Characteristic Communication Style Tendencies

| Tendency | Greater | | | Lesser |
|---|---|---|---|---|
| Tendency to use logic | S | C | D | I |
| Tendency to trust | I | S | D | C |
| Tendency to buy quickly | D | I | S | C |
| Tendency to be loyal | S | C | D | I |
| *D = Dominant; I = Influence; S = Steady; C = Compliant-to-Standards | | | | |

ments to fit your style as needed. Table 9.1 outlines the tendencies that are more or less characteristic of each of the basic communication styles.

The information shown in Figure 9.1 will guide you on how best to adapt your own style to another communication style. To use this, begin by finding your preferred communication style. Then identify the style of the other person or group, and identify the actions you can take to build rapport.

## Fear Underlies Why Individuals and Teams Do Not Resolve Conflict

Have you ever seen someone ignore an issue that is causing problems? This is a symptom of fear. When people do not know what to do or how to handle something, they often feel fear, which shuts them down.

We cannot resolve a conflict that we do not acknowledge. When we shut down, we stop seeing reality. The unconscious reaction is to lose clarity in our thinking, to go numb, and to blank out emotionally. We disengage, and we may not even realize we have done so, if our self-awareness is low. Giving in, passively submitting, acquiescing, or abdicating our own needs are symptoms of what we do when we are unconscious of or unwilling to acknowledge conflict.

Do you recall Bob from earlier? Bob was known for being passive–aggressive. He seemed to wear blinders to conflict, and he did not address issues with others directly. It was not uncommon for him to complain about people, but not speak

**FIGURE 9.1** How to Adapt Your Communication Style to Those of Others to Build Rapport

**Behavioral Communication Skills for Steady (S) Style Communicators**

| Step 1: Know yourself as a "S" person. | Step 2: Read the person you are speaking with. What style is that person using now? |
|---|---|
| • Natural salesperson, personable<br>• Steady and dependable<br>• Easily discouraged, low confidence<br>• Great on follow-through (may overservice)<br>• May give away $$$ under pressure<br>• More enthusiasm may be needed<br>• May overuse facts<br>• May wait too long to close | *Extroverted*     *Introverted*<br>Friendly: I     Cooperative: S<br>Direct: D     Analytical: C |

| Step 3: Use this chart when you are communicating with these types of people: | |
|---|---|
| **"D" Types** | **"S" Types** |
| "D" types are looking for: RESULTS<br><br>• Be confident; don't be intimidated.<br>• Close sooner than normal.<br>• Disagree with facts, not people.<br>• Do not be overpowered by them.<br>• Let them win (you win, too).<br>• Move faster than normal.<br>• Come on as strong as "D" is, but stay friendly. | "S" types are looking for: SECURITY<br><br>• Give them the facts.<br>• Provide the assurances they need.<br>• Be yourself.<br>• Close when you feel you have their trust.<br>• Assure them of the right decision.<br>• Introduce them to managers, service managers, etc.<br>• Follow up after sale. |
| **"I" Types** | **"C" Types** |
| "I" types are looking for: "THE EXPERIENCE"<br><br>• Allow them to talk, but keep focus.<br>• Provide them with minimal product knowledge.<br>• Provide follow-up.<br>• Give recognition.<br>• Listen to their stories.<br>• Have fun with them.<br>• "Jump" to close when ready. | "C" types are looking for: INFORMATION<br><br>• Answer questions with facts.<br>• Do not be too personal.<br>• Be direct and friendly.<br>• Do not touch.<br>• Give them their space.<br>• Do not fear their skeptical nature.<br>• Follow through on details.<br>• Give information, then close. |

directly to them. Bob did not allow himself to see or recognize conflicts in conversations, because he did not know how to identify and resolve conflict. Instead, he went into avoidance mode. When he would avoid dealing with the issue, tension would build in him. Over time this would be too much for him to deal with, and he would explode. Sometimes it was a loud outburst that stunned the other person. Bob had to learn how to notice what he was feeling, instead of ignoring his own feelings.

**FIGURE 9.1** How to Adapt Your Communication Style to Those of Others to Build Rapport *(continued)*

**Behavioral Communication Skills for Compliant (C) Style Communicators**

| Step 1: Know yourself as a "C" person. | Step 2: Read the person you are speaking with. What style is that person using now? |
|---|---|
| • Knows data<br>• May overuse data, overevaluate<br>• Needs more enthusiasm<br>• May have trouble selling products below their own standards<br>• Well organized<br>• Good service<br>• Analysis paralysis | *Extroverted*<br>Friendly: I<br>Direct: D<br><br>*Introverted*<br>Cooperative: S<br>Analytical: C |

| Step 3: Use this chart when you are communicating with these types of people: | |
|---|---|
| **"D" Types** | **"S" Types** |
| "D" types are looking for: RESULTS<br><br>• Touch upon high points of facts and figures.<br>• Do not overprovide data.<br>• Move quickly.<br>• Be brief, to the point.<br>• Satisfy their strong ego.<br>• Allow them to "win" (you win, too). | "S" types are looking for: SECURITY<br><br>• Move slowly.<br>• Provide facts and figures.<br>• Do not overcontrol or be too pushy.<br>• Provide assurances.<br>• Develop trust.<br>• Focus on reliability and service.<br>• Allow personal talk. |
| **"I" Types** | **"C" Types** |
| "I" types are looking for: "THE EXPERIENCE"<br><br>• Focus on people, be friendly and fun.<br>• Listen to them as they talk.<br>• Ask questions.<br>• Show excitement about products.<br>• Close earlier than normal. | "C" types are looking for: INFORMATION<br><br>• Give data.<br>• Remain in control.<br>• Examine positives and negatives.<br>• Close earlier than you would expect.<br>• Follow through on promises.<br>• Provide evidence. |

His self-awareness needed to grow. When he noticed the first symptoms of anger in his body and his thinking, he needed to ask himself: "What crossed my boundaries? Whom do I speak with to ask for what I need in this situation?" When Bob noticed the first symptoms of fear, he needed to ask himself: "What is causing this fear? Is this a signal that I need to slow down or that I do not know how to do what needs to be done next? Am I avoiding speaking to someone, based on half-truths or misinformation? How could I create a conversation with that person to deal with what needs to be discussed, so we do not ignore this, causing it to get bigger?" Guiding Bob to develop

**FIGURE 9.1** How to Adapt Your Communication Style to Those of Others to Build Rapport *(continued)*

### Behavioral Communication Skills for Dominant (D) Style Communicators

| Step 1: Know yourself as a "D" person. | Step 2: Read the person you are speaking with. What style is that person using now? |
|---|---|
| • Results oriented<br>• Wants to close fast<br>• Argumentative<br>• May try to overpower the person<br>• Likes to win<br>• May not follow up properly<br>• May be unprepared<br>• Can handle several customers at once | *Extroverted*　　*Introverted*<br>Friendly: I　　Cooperative: S<br>Direct: D　　Analytical: C |

| Step 3: Use this chart when you are communicating with these types of people: | |
|---|---|
| **"D" Types** | **"S" Types** |
| "D" types are looking for: RESULTS<br><br>• Be direct.<br>• Give alternatives.<br>• Make sure you let them win (make sure you win, too).<br>• Disagree with facts.<br>• Enjoy the "combat" (good match).<br>• Don't try to build a friendship.<br>• Do not dictate to them.<br>• Move quickly; they decide fast.<br>• Do not try to overpower them. | "S" types are looking for: SECURITY<br><br>• Slow down presentation.<br>• Build trust.<br>• People focus.<br>• Give them the facts they need.<br>• Give a logical presentation.<br>• Get "little" agreements.<br>• Listen carefully.<br>• Show sincerity in presentation.<br>• Don't control or dominate.<br>• Do not close fast. |
| **"I" Types** | **"C" Types** |
| "I" types are looking for: "THE EXPERIENCE"<br><br>• Be personal, friendly.<br>• Slow down, take time.<br>• Joke around and have fun.<br>• Allow them to talk.<br>• Provide recognition.<br>• Don't talk down to them.<br>• Talk about people.<br>• Follow up often. | "C" types are looking for: INFORMATION<br><br>• Give them the data.<br>• Do not touch.<br>• Be patient, slow.<br>• Use flyers with data.<br>• Give more info than you'd like.<br>• Keep control.<br>• Do not talk personally.<br>• Do not be pushy. |

emotional intelligence was the first step in helping him to deal with conflict. After several months of coaching, Bob stopped letting fear of past conflicts shut him down to conflict.

Interpersonal fear, irrational beliefs about failure, groupthink, problematic power dynamics, and information hoarding cause people to avoid resolving conflicts and sharing their learning with others. These patterns create conflict in teams and across teams. Leaders can change this pattern by facilitating

**FIGURE 9.1** How to Adapt Your Communication Style to Those of Others to Build Rapport (continued)

### Behavioral Communication Skills for Influence (I) Style Communicators

| Step 1: Know yourself as a "I" person. | Step 2: Read the person you are speaking with. What style is that person using now? |
|---|---|
| • Social<br>• People-oriented lack of attention to detail<br>• May overpromise<br>• May be too talkative<br>• May close too slowly or not at all<br>• Enthusiastic<br>• Wordy, nonlogical presentation | *Extroverted*<br>Friendly: I<br>Direct: D<br><br>*Introverted*<br>Cooperative: S<br>Analytical: C |

| Step 3: Use this chart when you are communicating with these types of people: | |
|---|---|
| **"D" Types** | **"S" Types** |
| "D" types are looking for: RESULTS<br><br>• Do not touch.<br>• Stay business-like.<br>• Be direct and to the point.<br>• Do not overpromise.<br>• Do not joke.<br>• Let them win (you win, too).<br>• Confidently close, not allowing them to overpower you. | "S" types are looking for: SECURITY<br><br>• Give them the facts.<br>• Slow down.<br>• Be friendly, personal and earn their trust.<br>• Provide assurances of your promises.<br>• Get "little" agreements.<br>• Let them talk; you ask questions.<br>• Take necessary time before closing.<br>• Follow up after the sale. |
| **"I" Types** | **"C" Types** |
| "I" types are looking for: "THE EXPERIENCE"<br><br>• Have fun.<br>• Don't waste too much time talking.<br>• Make sure you close.<br>• Give them the recognition.<br>• Let them talk more than you. | "C" types are looking for: INFORMATION<br><br>• Keep your distance.<br>• Do not touch.<br>• Give them the facts, figures, and proof.<br>• Do not waste time.<br>• Do not be personal.<br>• Be friendly and direct.<br>• Answer all questions, then close.<br>• Be concerned with details. |

open sharing meetings, creating safety, and rewarding people for overcoming defensive interpersonal dynamics that inhibit the sharing of ideas. High-performing teams help organizations realize the benefits and learning from both success and failure when they overcome their fears and move to being passionate about a common igniting purpose.

When you are focused on creating something you really want, you are coming from love, joy, and passion. When you avoid conflict, you are acting out of fear. There is a difference between avoiding conflict (coming from fear) and, on the other end of the scale, being so focused on what you want to create that you do not put energy into issues that take you from your goal. There are certain negative triggers that we are wise to avoid by redirecting ourselves back to our own "That's for Me!" lists, and thus putting more energy into creating joy, passion, and love as our emotional set point. Focusing on what we want to create means leaving behind what we do not want, and sometimes others may think we are avoiding an issue when, in fact, we've moved beyond it. Only you know the difference for yourself. And sometimes we have to deal with a conflict to move a group forward, so they can get unstuck from fear and be able to achieve desired results. The difference is that, in avoiding conflict, the underlying emotion is fear. Stop the fear-based behaviors, and deal with the real issues, so you can move your goals and projects forward.

What are you resisting? Stop and answer that question. Whatever pops up for you when you ask that question is likely something you are avoiding. Is that something where you have unresolved fear? Is there a conflict under that issue? Is there something you have been avoiding dealing with? If so, that is a signal that there is a fear-based conflict that has not yet been resolved.

When people fight about something, the subject of the argument is rarely the real issue. Typically, the real issue is about feelings of vulnerability, connectedness, safety, fear, lack of trust, or love. Emotional states fuel conflict, so being unaware of feelings can lead to unconscious conflicts.

Instead of being afraid that we do not know how to do something, we can create a new story. We can remind ourselves of the complex things we have learned how to do in the past. We can find a mentor or role model who knows how to do what we need to learn now. Do you recall Jacqueline? That was the situation she was in.

## Jacqueline's Story (Continued from Chapter 5)

Jacqueline was a senior manager who realized that the owner of the company where she works, Ben, had her in a box. Ben labeled Jacqueline as being "too aggressive, arrogant, and defensive" after he received feedback from her employees that she was difficult to report to. Jacqueline had to learn how to collaborate. She was the most knowledgeable person in her department. She knew how to solve complex problems and had deep expertise. The problem was that she did not let her team members or her peers share their thinking. She would jump in and emphatically say what needed to be done without reading her audience. She left no room for others to cocreate and partner with her. As a result she was being held back from promotions that would take her into larger leadership roles. Initially, Jacqueline did not understand the conflicts she was creating for her team members, who felt she did not listen to them or care about developing them. From her 360 survey, it became clear to her that collaboration, listening, and including others in solving problems would be necessary for her to move through the conflict she was creating for others. As Jacqueline began to practice people reading and adapting her style to the situation, as she practiced deep listening, things changed for her. She allowed people to work through problems and to discuss their ideas; she began to be a trusted partner who helped people work through conflicts. After a few months, Ben began to hear new feedback that Jacqueline was now collaborating.

## Conflict Management Is a Business Issue

Jim Haudan, the CEO of Root Learning and author of *The Art of Engagement: Bridging the Gap Between People and Possibilities*, describes what he calls the disengagement canyon that exists in companies between managers and workers. He gives voices to the people in the trenches and imagines them explaining their disengagement in these ways:

- I can't be engaged if I'm overwhelmed. Too many corporate directives are coming at me, and I have no idea what the priorities really are.
- I can't be engaged if I don't get it. When the strategy is not relevant to me, I don't get it, and I do not understand why we are doing what we are told to do.
- I can't be engaged if I'm scared. We are taught to be guarded, cautious, and restrained so as not to risk losing our jobs or reputations, and thus it is not safe to learn new skills. We'd have to reveal what we don't know and admit vulnerability.
- I can't be engaged if I don't see the big picture. Leaders keep sending one puzzle piece at a time, telling what to do, and I don't know how to connect the pieces to understand what we are really creating and why.
- I can't be engaged if it's not mine. Involve me and I'll understand.
- I can't be engaged if my leaders don't face reality. Unless we are in regular conversations with each other, we create unacknowledged canyons between what managers and doers are focused on, and there is no alignment.

Can you relate to any of these voices? They explain the unresolved conflicts underlying many people's actions and why they do not engage in collaboration. Often people do not realize their frustrations and complaints are unresolved conflicts looking for a resolution.

In each voice there is a resignation that is avoiding speaking up to resolve an underlying conflict. To resolve these conflicts, we first have to allow ourselves to recognize them and ask questions such as: What can I do to keep my cool when things aren't going the way I hoped they would? How can I turn the situation around, create new solutions to the problems, and get back on track? Creating this type of change involves knowing how to craft conversations to deal with breakdowns and then to resolve the conflicts.

In *Teaming: How Organizations Learn, Innovate, and Compete in the Knowledge Economy*, Professor Amy Edmondson of Harvard Business School shares how leaders and organizations are approaching the increasing complexity in problems and conflicts they face. The mindset of execution, which is focused on telling people what to do in order to get things done, was successful in the past. In an increasingly competitive global economy a different approach is needed. Organizations now must learn how to deal with complexity and resolve conflict by collaborating in teams.

Cultural and thinking differences, the reality of hierarchical status, or distance can separate team members. Leaders can close these gaps by understanding the existence of the obstacles, seeing the resulting conflicts, and then adapting their style to support and facilitate teaming successfully. The seeds of the solution are to maximize learning across groups within a business.

## Maximizing Learning Across Networks

To maximize learning, both conflict and failure are necessary. Successful team members and businesses know that complexity and conflict go hand in hand. And they share a belief that "we can work through this to a resolution." Persistence in problem solving occurs when leaders create an environment of safety, an environment where it is OK—even expected—to identify problems, voice concerns, and deal openly with conflict. For example, leaders could say: "This is a complex issue, and none of us knows how to solve it yet. Thus, we'll all need to put our puzzle pieces out to examine them together and then explore ways to fit them together to see what possible solutions emerge. It is not likely that we will all see things the same way, and I want to encourage us to keep talking through those situations." When your leader asks you to do this, come forward and engage by sharing your ideas and suggestions directly. Learning thoughtfully from failures and sharing organizational knowledge is essential for continuous improvement and innovation, no matter whether you are a leader, peer, or team member.

> For over a century, we've focused too much on relentless execution and depended too much on fear to get things done. That era is over. Human and organizational obstacles to teaming and learning can be overcome. Few of today's most pressing social problems can be solved within the four walls of any organization, no matter how enlightened or extraordinary. Generating ideas to solve problems is the currency of the future; teaming is the way to develop, implement, and improve those ideas.
> —Amy Edmondson

Organizations thrive, or fail to thrive, based on how well small groups communicate through conflict. In most organizations, teams carry out the work that produces value for customers. These teams need to know how to embrace and communicate through conflict and then share their learning with the larger organization.

Organizations learn when flexible, fluid collaborations are encouraged across teams, departments, and then the whole organization. The problem is that teams, and other dynamic groups, don't naturally share their learning. They often hide conflicts. People are also more likely to hoard and hide their mistakes and the learning from those mistakes. They do not want others to see what has been amassed from mistakes and conflict. Avoiding conflict does not create success and hampers organizational learning.

## Conversations for Breakdown: Acknowledging That It's Not Going the Way We Wanted

A conflict is not necessarily evidenced by a fight. It may be lurking underneath the surface in a relationship. The energy used to keep it submerged could instead be used to create something better. If we are not stepping up to deal with unresolved conflict on the teams we lead, the team members will lose respect for our management capabilities. Respect from others often comes once they know that we will deal with conflict in solutions-focused ways.

The most successful collaborators seek to understand the other side's concerns and needs as much as they seek to understand and share their own. They ask questions and carefully listen, so that the other person sees their willingness to be in a mutual exploration and solution-focused conversation. It can be debilitating to be filled with fear or anger from unacknowledged conflict or an issue that is habitually ignored. We cannot make others collaborate when they are unwilling to do so, but we can invite them to explore what is the effect of seeing new possibilities, even if they are resistant to it.

Many years ago, I stumbled upon several questions that have been a powerful tool when I'm collaborating with others, especially with people who have communication styles different from mine. These questions enable me to dig up unresolved conflict, so that we can clean it up. I now ask these questions every few months to see if there is anything that has gotten stuck and needs to be acknowledged. I ask one of the following questions to get the conversation going:

- Is there anything that is in the way of us working together in a high-performing manner?
- If you are holding onto resentment, bitterness, or anger about anything related to our work together, could we discuss it?
- Is there anything you'd like me to ask forgiveness for that I have not addressed?

Setting up a conversation like this clears the air. It enables me to apologize for anything that I may have done unknowingly that has caused conflict for the other person in working with me. This is a useful conversation to hold with key stakeholders in your role at least every 10 to 12 months. Do not have this conversation just before review time; then it will seem like it is a test and not sincerely meant to build strong rapport and trust in the relationship. The purpose of creating this conversation is to sincerely understand the other person's perspective and feelings and to take action on what she says, because you are willing to be influenced by her. Carefully listen. When someone feels like you are willing to be influenced by her words, then she will be more willing to be influenced by you.

And sometimes, despite our best efforts, we land in a breakdown, where things are not working; we are oscillating with no results. These can be painful times. Acknowledging that we are in this state is useful. Admitting we are in a breakdown can cause us to let go of resistance. Good collaborators know the power of creating a conversation for acknowledging breakdown. Use a conversation for breakdown in the following situations:

- You notice yourself or someone else caught in circular thinking.
- You feel jammed up, unable to think clearly, stuck, or afraid.
- You are not meeting goals.
- You are unclear about what to do next.
- You notice a values conflict that is not able to be resolved.

### Phrases and Questions to Engage Someone in a Conversation in Order to Acknowledge a Breakdown

Things are not going as we thought they would. I feel stuck. Do you also?

We have a commitment to do XYZ, but it feels like we are only focused on ABC, and we can't seem to get moving in the right direction. What actions do we need to take to produce the desired results? What is it that is keeping us from moving forward and doing what we need to do? With whom could we talk in order to resolve this?

If someone else were looking at this situation, would he say we were spinning around in circles, oscillating instead of moving forward?

Let's take two days as a break from the intensity of this situation and let this sit. Then let's both meet, ready to discuss how we are going to move forward. At that meeting we will make a decision on what our top priorities really are, identifying what cannot be done as well as what will be done given our current reality. OK?

After a conversation that acknowledges a breakdown, it is often time to have a conversation for conflict resolution to address what was under the breakdown and move forward.

## Conversations for Conflict Resolution

If we work in a corporate culture that does not support conflict resolution, we will not likely have the kind of collaboration that brings innovation and creates future wealth. When people are afraid of differing ideas or conflict and they do not know how to communicate about differences of opinions, then their differences in interpretations of reality, intuition, and feelings squash creativity and innovation. This can be turned around with a well-crafted conversation for resolution. First we need to identify what type of conflict we are dealing with.

### Types of Conflicts

Me-me conflict—me against myself

Me-you conflict—me against another

Me-them conflict—me against or feeling caught in the middle of a group

Me–team conflict—me against a team or department

Me–big group conflict—me against others across several departments or teams or my team against another team

It is wise to create a conversation for conflict resolution in these situations:

There are chronic tensions in a relationship.

You feel anger, resentment, or bitterness.

You sense someone else is feeling anger, resentment, or bitterness towards you.

You sense someone is afraid to speak up.

You are disappointed with the results and outcomes in working with a team member, peer, boss, client, or colleague.

Someone is ignoring an issue that is important to you.

You are ignoring an issue that someone keeps bringing up to you over and over, and you wonder why.

I am frequently asked, "How can I begin a conversation to deal with a conflict without shutting the other person down?" These phrases and questions are a good way to begin addressing conflicts that have limited collaboration and held back desired results:

I have a commitment to focus on the desired outcomes we'd like to create. I've noticed that in the past I (and perhaps we) seemed to focus on what was wrong. We talked about the problem over and over. Now I am going to shift this pattern and instead speak about and focus on the desired state, the fulfillment of the goals. Will you join me in doing this?

I'd like to hear your perspectives on XYZ. When would be a good time to discuss these issues so that we can really hear each other's ideas? Perhaps if we set up two meetings a few days apart to focus on this issue, it will give us time to reflect on and build on each other's ideas. Would you be willing to do that?

I'd like to hear more about how you came to this conclusion. Would you share more details with me here so I have the back story on this? Perhaps if I understood that, I would then come to the same conclusions as you.

Is there something we are avoiding, tiptoeing around, that if addressed, would help us move forward productively?

We may see things differently here, and I would like to explore what we agree on and where we are seeing things differently. Would you be willing to start with what we currently agree on related to XYZ?

I have a conflict with myself that I've been stuck in, and I'd like to talk it out with someone who is unbiased. Would you be willing to ask me questions and help me unravel this, so I can figure out what I am really feeling rather than staying stuck?

I'd like to invite you to have coffee with me off-site next week. I am struggling with something, and I would really appreciate the opportunity to discuss it with you to get your input on this issue.

Sometimes it is useful to agree to disagree and then move on without holding resentment or bitterness. I'm wondering are we in one of those situations? Are we both able to move on and let this issue go so it is not preventing us from doing the next action?

I'm committed to cocreating a resolution to this issue with you. How would you suggest we proceed from here so that we ensure we have heard each other and have been thoughtful about how to move forward?

## Common Mistakes in Resolving Conflict

The most common mistake people make when faced with conflict is to avoid it entirely and then become bitter and resentful that things did not go their way. This is how victim stories become patterns. When we stuff our feelings down inside without dealing with them, we are creating bigger problems for ourselves. Avoidance and silence do not resolve conflicts. If you have had three or more instances of thinking about something troubling you, then it is time to address it, so you can gain clarity about how you want to resolve the issue.

Take a look at what can happen when we don't address conflict. Bob did allow conflict to be expressed. As a result, he did not understand why not much changed around him. He did not get the attention he wanted from his own boss, and there was little collaboration going on with his team, because he avoided letting ideas bubble up in team meetings. Bob was afraid his team members or his boss would disagree with him or each other, and he did not know how to handle the conversation when this happened. When differences of opinions were expressed and conflicts bubbled up in a team meeting, Bob would say, "The two of you can take that off line; we do not need to spend more time on it now." The two people he is referring to were peers, and they wanted his guidance and input on how to proceed, but he squashed these discussions too quickly, so that resolution was not possible. He never circled back to ask the two other people to meet with him on the issue. The ironic part of this is that, though Bob was conflict avoidant, he was swimming in a sea of unresolved conflict around him.

After coaching and practice in using these new skills, Bob learned how to address issues as they came up, make a decision together with his team, and move forward, focused on what the cocreated resolution would be. Bob is no longer struggling to lead his team effectively, because he learned how to communicate through conflicts to create resolutions with his team.

I taught Bob that dismissing or not listening to issues that someone wants to express is a mistake that may happen because someone is conflict avoidant or because he thinks the person raising the issue is below him, out of line, or not worthy of attention. When the person who is not being heard is a stakeholder in your work or on your team, there will be an undercurrent of conflict that limits people's engagement. Signs of an undercurrent of conflict that can sabotage collaboration include:

Dancing on eggshells, not speaking clearly about what issues exist

Making sarcastic or snide comments

Resorting to screaming and bullying

Making cheap shots that come out sideways instead of directly addressing the issue

Not asking for what you want, not being clear on your own desires, and instead waiting for someone else to state what he wants is another classic mistake that leads to resentment over time.

Another mistake that people make in conflict resolution is not paying attention to differences in communication styles and motivators. When we expect someone else to use our style all the time, we are creating stress for him. By accepting and discussing our differences in our preferred styles, by playing to the strengths of both our styles, and by working through the natural differences, we will have stronger collaboration and better results.

## Conversations to Withdraw and Disengage: When It's Just Not Working

It is unrealistic to think that all relationships will be enjoyable, friendly, or productive forever. We do not have the time to have deeply meaningful work relationships with every person we see and work with. Business and professional relationships will shift and change over time. When we are working closely on a project together, we may collaborate regularly. We achieve the desired results, and then we move off that project. We may not see a person again for months or years. We want to keep the door open to work together again without wondering if there was an unresolved issue. For this reason, it is useful to create a conversation for closure when a project ends.

Business relationships can also deteriorate for a wide variety of reasons. The most common reasons are loss of trust, respect, or integrity. These problems usually result from a lack of understanding of another's communication style and workplace motivators, or from low emotional intelligence. Sometimes we have to admit to ourselves that we are in a toxic, one-sided, or unhealthy relationship that is causing more problems than it is worth. When we are in "fix him" mode, we are enmeshed. We need to stop and change the dynamics of the relationship. Sometimes it is best to end a relationship with a team or boss so that we have time to work with a more fulfilling one.

A coaching client called me recently to talk through a challenge he was facing. He reports to the CEO of a public company. My client, let's call him Dave, believes his boss is doing something unethical—misallocating company funds. As a result, Dave had a conversation with his boss to calmly ask about the issue. Dave was careful not to indicate that he thought the CEO's behavior was intentional; he suggested that this was an oversight that could be corrected. Dave's boss responded with anger and claimed that his choice was not a misallocation. The boss said, "It is perfectly fine to do what I am doing." Dave had already spoken with the corporate attorney to ask hypothetically whether the action was acceptable without revealing that the CEO was currently doing it. The general counsel told Dave the act was illegal. Dave gave this information to the CEO. A few days later Dave was told his office was being moved out of the senior executive team area—away from the CEO. Dave's office was moved back into another building and assignments were taken from him. This is an example of a values clash that creates a conflict. It appears the CEO believes he is above the rules and now does not want input from Dave anymore. This is a breakdown that will not be resolved in a conversation between Dave and the CEO.

If you are permanently shut down around someone and feel uncomfortable in that person's company, no matter what you have done to improve the situation, you are likely in a toxic relationship. Behavior that is unethical or physical and emotional abuses are automatic walk-away signs. If you are questioning whether a relationship fits into this area for you, it probably does.

For example, Alex was in her first job and wanted to please Karen, her new boss. Karen had just been promoted to supervisor after a year in the organization. Alex had been hired by the HR department and was now reporting to Karen. In their first two weeks working together, Alex noticed Karen would scream loudly at people in front of peers. Karen seemed to play games, saying she would agree to something and then at the last minute not allow it, and then laugh harshly at the people involved. Karen also refused to acknowledge some of the people on the team by name. Karen would talk badly about others on the team to their peers. Alex noticed that Karen was mean-spirited, refusing to engage with some people because of their nationalities. When Karen told her she should not say the names of these team members as a way to ignore them, Alex realized how unhealthy the situation was. Alex had to interact with these same people frequently to get her work done, and she was feeling torn by this crazy relationship with her new boss. It can be a long road to repair a relationship that suffers from emotional abuse like this. It is not always worth the emotional investment it takes to resolve it. My advice to Alex was to find a new position and to inform HR of the problems in her exit interview. This was being solution-focused in this situation.

In situations like this we can move out of sadness when we learn from the experience. The learning for Alex was this: it is important to interview your boss to see if you want to work for him or her. Not every opportunity to collaborate will be right for you. Look closely to see whether the project, department, and organization are a good fit for you. Be willing to leave when you are in a situation that will squash your self-esteem and growth.

## In Action: Jane Dolente

Jane Dolente, the managing principal at The Skilled Negotiator shared with me her experiences regarding conflict resolution:

> I was hired to help the employees of a city government improve their customer-service skills. City employees, especially building inspectors, were often adversarial with their customers. When a building inspector condemned a property used by drug dealers and pimps as a base of operations, angry confrontations ensued. The inspectors believed the job put their lives at risk. They believed in power and intimidation, not collaboration to solve problems. Nevertheless, the new mayor wanted to reduce conflict and upgrade the city's image, so the inspectors were required to take the training.
>
> During one of the workshops, George, a frustrated building inspector, exploded, saying, "This training is an insulting waste of time." He threatened to leave and take the rest of the participants with him. The group waited for my reaction. I could take the bait and get into a power struggle or keep my cool, create a conversation for conflict resolution and collaborate. It occurred to me that I was in the kind of confrontation that they faced every day. I needed to show deep listening.
>
> I turned to the other participants and said: "My customer, George, is upset and he has a right to be. From his perspective this

class is a waste of his time. What I say and do next matters. You handle upset, angry customers every day. How should I respond? Should I play the expert and overpower him or is there an opportunity to collaborate?"

I let the group coach me. We ran experiments. One participant played the angry drug dealer and another played the city inspector. We saw that anger breeds more anger in conflict. Emotions are contagious. We saw that positive emotions can be contagious too. We saw that listening and empathy had surprising power to enable a conversation to move forward during conflict.

Not everyone was sold on the power of collaboration, but we weakened the business-is-war ideology in the minds of most. George not only stayed in the class, he later wrote a letter of recommendation about the training. I could not have dreamed of a better outcome. My belief in working together through conflict to create collaboration grew deeper roots that day. Thank you, George!

## Conflict Resolution Application Exercise

High-performing teams help organizations realize the benefits and learning from both success and failure when they overcome their fears and move to being passionate about a common igniting purpose. Think about an existing conflict you want to resolve. Ask yourself:

What is the igniting purpose that connects you?

How could you communicate with the peer, boss, or team about this?

Now, can you identify another conflict that is affecting you as a peer, an employee, or a leader?

Related to that, answer these questions:

What is it that you want to create instead of what is currently happening?

Who has the decision-making authority to change the current reality?

What are that person or team's communication style and motivators?

What does that person or team currently think of the conflict or issue?

What could you say to share your perspective?

How could you craft a conversation for conflict resolution to engage the right person or people?

When could you schedule a time to have this conversation?

# CHAPTER 10

# Relationship Building

## Building Your Collaboration and Networking Map

You are now ready to begin building a collaboration map. This map will be so valuable that you will be using it for a long time. The map will bring together all the ideas discussed so far, and it will help you see your community of possible collaborators in new ways.

Successful leaders have an ability to spot opportunity and to know whom to tap to get things done. These qualities depend on the ability to people read and use a set of strategic networking skills that you will develop by doing this activity.

You will build a map that will show three distinct groups with whom you can collaborate:

1. **Today's job tasks:** people who work in your organization and are focused on the day-to-day goals you are working toward.
2. **Kindred spirits:** people with whom you work well, who have common goals and inspirations; colleagues with whom you enjoy connecting to grow and share inspiration.

3. **Strategic big picture:** leaders who will ask you questions, challenge your thinking, and help you see the future for your career, organization, and industry.

By interacting regularly with people from these three groups, you will begin to see new opportunities and how to capitalize on them. You will be able to leverage your network of contacts to move projects and ideas forward. You will implement what is on your "That's for Me!" list with more ease.

## Jose's Story

When Jose Steele became the new operations manager of and partner in a mid-sized company, he was not thinking about building a collaboration map. He had been asked to take a turn-around assignment that he knew would be very challenging. He was given an equity stake in the business, and for the first time in his career he was part of a senior leadership team. Though Jose understood this role would demand more time from him than he had ever given to any job before, he did not fully understand his new role as a leader. He only thought about how to master the day-to-day tasks involved in his new job. He was so focused on his internal workflow that he stayed in his office in front of his computer much of the time. Instead of interacting with people in all aspects of the business, he sent hundreds of daily e-mails to the same small group. Occasionally, he would attend a team meeting, but he primarily met with the same five or ten people over and over.

To Jose the idea of creating a collaboration and networking map was a waste of time. Jose thought of networking as a dirty, manipulative task, focused only on trading favors. "Schmoozing with people" was not a skill Jose thought he needed.

Do you know anyone like Jose?

Jose moved from being in a technical role to being in a leadership role, but he did not see the leadership transition he was going through while he was in it. He missed the signals that he would need to change the way he was operating in his work. His maturity level did not evolve to the level of his new position. Eventually, this new job demanded that Jose rethink what it meant for him to be an effective leader and partner in a firm that wanted to grow and be recognized as a player in the industry.

This was the time Jose most needed a network of potential collaborators. Jose needed support, feedback, resources, information, and new insights about the industry for him to do his job well. Now that Jose was challenged to move beyond his functional area of expertise and look at the larger strategic issues that come with being on a senior leadership team, he was struggling. He did not understand that success in his role was more about relationship building than it was about his analytical ability. Jose needed to realize that building a useful collaboration and networking map would be vital to his success and was therefore the real work of his new job. Fortunately, the president of the company understood the kind of skills Jose would need for his new role, which is why he asked me to work with Jose one-on-one. The president wanted me to guide Jose in learning how to delegate effectively and collaborate with a wider group of people.

In my first meeting with Jose, he told me that creating a collaborating and networking map would be "manipulative—just a tool to use people." As we looked together at his schedule for the past several weeks, it was clear that the people he had engaged with recently were only those in his organization who were important in the short term to the routine of daily operations. As we dug deeper, it was also clear that Jose had avoided collaborating and networking outside his group, because he was uncomfortable starting conversations with people he did not know or with whom he had no formal reason to discuss a project. He was not seeing the strategic needs of his business as a driver for building new relationships. Jose's attitude was not a surprise to me. I have seen this mistake made frequently by people who have emphasized building technical competencies

221

to a mastery level at the expense of building relationships. These people think that they will be recognized for their mastery, and they miss the importance of being able to grow an organization with talented people for the long term. Jose's resistance shifted as I asked him questions about effective senior leaders in his organization. He began to describe how he had recently become aware that his boss has high-quality relationships, based on mutual trust, across several organizations and in every part of the industry. For the first time, Jose realized that his boss's power and influence as a leader came from these diverse relationships.

I explained to Jose that one of the mistakes with relying on a network that is solely focused on today's tasks—on the objectives that are in front of one now—is that one then avoids thinking about the big strategic questions such as: "What do I enjoy doing? What are the right actions for the company to be taking to grow in our industry? How can I play to my strengths while guiding the organization's growth? Who else do I want to involve in expanding the mission of our organization? How can I develop star performers, so we are expanding our capabilities?"

As a professional moves into a new role, his or her network of collaborators will need to be reviewed and expanded, both internally and externally. A network of high-performing collaborators will need to be developed. In fact, this may be the most important first step when taking a new assignment.

I encouraged Jose to identify people he would enjoy connecting with, kindred spirits outside his organization. At that point, he confessed that he was not comfortable with his social skills. Meeting new people did not come easily to Jose, and he had not learned how to people read. I taught him how to identify communication styles, motivators, and the current tone of emotion in a conversation. I asked Jose to identify professional associations and conferences, clubs, and alumni groups. Then I encouraged him to think about personal-interest groups he might want to invite others to participate in. My assignment to Jose was to spend five hours per week focused on people reading and building new relationships outside his own office. I suggested, "As you people read, be open to sharing information, ideas, referrals, and support, such as mentoring or specific coaching with the new people you meet."

Within three months, Jose had meaningful new connections for himself and his organization. He was visibly excited when he showed me his list of gatherings he had been attending and the people he added to his collaborating and networking map. He also showed me how he used LinkedIn to identify people who had a link to someone he wanted to meet. Jose became more comfortable picking up the phone and calling the person who was linked to a person he wanted to meet. He would explain why he wanted to meet the new person and ask if his connection would be willing to make an introduction. Clearly, Jose's social skills were improving.

Jose also used LinkedIn in other ways to expand his opportunities for collaborating. He learned how to use the Question and Answer tools, and was now communicating this way with a wide group of people in his industry. Jose even used LinkedIn to review the backgrounds of people that would be in meetings. Prior to attending a meeting, he would examine their LinkedIn profiles to help him identify questions that would spark meaningful conversations. His interest in the conversations he was having fired him up so that he was no longer focused on feeling nervous or afraid when meeting new people. Jose's mastery of a new technical tool (LinkedIn) combined with his new skills in people reading fueled his enthusiasm for building his collaboration map.

Three months after we began working together, Jose told me how amazing his boss really was, now that Jose realized what his boss was doing. Jose had just attended a conference with his boss, and while there Jose identified some people from an organization that his boss wanted to learn more about. Jose introduced himself while at a breakout session and set up a meeting with his boss later in the day. He could see how his boss was a strategic player in the industry because of the relationships he had built over time. Jose was now beginning to develop this ability for himself. Jose was maturing.

At our next meeting, Jose told me he had just been given a larger team of people to manage. On the top of the list of items to discuss with his new team members, Jose had written: "Share the importance of helping team members to see the moments when they will need to challenge their perspective on what is most important to their long-term success. Discuss how they manage their time—show them how to build a collaborating and networking map."

"What makes a collaborating and networking map so powerful is the referral potential and the ability to help people in meaningful ways," Jose told his team members. Jose now had a new skill in his tool kit, and he was teaching it to others. He recognized that, for him to delegate effectively so he had time for larger strategic issues, Jose would need to identify a pool of people under him who wanted to grow. Jose made a list of all his projects and identified who would be ready to take on various aspects of his work. Delegating tasks would make more time available for him to do other things. Jose's perspective on how he added value had now fully shifted to being a leader, a developer of others; he was operating from a more strategic mindset, because of his realizations about the collaborating and networking map.

As I watched Jose transform over the next six months, I saw that he was no longer hiding in his own department, but now creating allies in peer positions. He had even begun to think about how he could influence who was being interviewed for the open board position in his organization, and he had nominated one of his key stakeholders for a special award in his industry. He knew these actions were deepening his relationships and trust in important ways.

## Creating Your Map

There are two options for how to begin to create your own map, and the option you choose will depend on how your brain likes to sort information. Choose the option that you are drawn to.

Begin by opening your spreadsheet software and creating a new spreadsheet called the "Collaborating and Networking Map."

Begin by getting a stack of three differently colored Post-it notes and a huge blank wall where you will be able to hang the Post-it notes as you create your map.

What you will do next includes a combination of these steps:

Write the name of a person who is a key stakeholder to your work (in the first column or on a Post-it note).

Identify what you exchange—how you help each other (in the next column or on that same Post-it note).

On a scale from 1 (not high) to 10 (very high) rate your level of trust—your tie to this person.

Identify how you met—who introduced you to each other? If it was you, write "Me."

Based on your experience with this person, what is his or her preferred communication style?

What are his or her top motivators? What is the emotional wake that has formed in your relationship?

Is there a maturity level that shows up in your interactions with this person?

Do this over and over, until you have done it for each of the key stakeholders in your network. Color code groups within your network so that all the people who work in your company are highlighted or on yellow Post-its—or choose whatever colors you like best. All the people you met at your industry association meeting are highlighted together or are on blue Post-its. All the people in your family are on pink Post-its. Do this for each of the key groups in your network.

Use LinkedIn to identify additional people in your current network.

If you are using spreadsheet software, put your name at the top of the list of everyone in your network. Rank the people based on how close your connection is with them. The person who is further from you is less of a connection.

If you are using Post-it notes on a wall, put your own name on a Post-it note in the middle of the wall. Then place the other Post-it notes around your name, based on how close the connection you share is. In other words, the people you know only remotely will be farther away around the circle you are creating than those who are your close friends. It will look like a colorful map on the wall with concentric circles around you.

Now stand back from this far enough so that you can identify who the network brokers, connectors, and super-connectors are. These are the people who have introduced you to the most number of people in your network. Who jumps out at you? Are you intentionally creating opportunities to converse with your high connectors?

Next, capture how you have brokered information or ideas for others. In what ways have you given back or helped others? How could you add value to others going forward? In what ways do you most enjoy giving and sharing your expertise?

What are you realizing from doing this activity? Take time to reflect on your map and the new insights that arise from seeing your map.

Lynda Gratton is a professor of management practice at the London Business School. She is a leading authority on people in organizations and the future of work. In her book *Hot Spots: Why Some Teams, Workplaces and Organizations Buzz with Energy—*

*and Others Don't,* she introduced the idea of "organizational hot spots"—areas of highly engaged and innovative activity. Imagine being able to look at your collaborating and networking map with thermal goggles that show where the energy between people and teams flares—where people are deeply engaged in creating exciting and meaningful new possibilities. We are moving from a business world based on competition to one that is based on collaboration and shared purpose, and your map will enable you to see whether you are moving toward high-energy connections.

This is Lynda Gratton's formula for creating a high-energy field that fuels collaboration:

Hot Spots = (Cooperative Mindset × Boundary Spanning × Igniting Purpose) × Productive Capacity

In this formula, a cooperative mindset, boundary spanning, and an igniting purpose have a multiplicative effect on each other. The lack of any one of these three elements significantly reduces the potential energy of a hot spot. Let's explore each of these three areas.

A cooperative mindset develops as a result of self-fulfilling thought patterns. Your thought patterns (your beliefs) create the design of your habits of behavior, which leads you to be either open-minded or close-minded. When working with other people, a cooperative mindset is necessary to achieve effective collaboration. Research shows that the emergence of a cooperative mindset is determined by the leaders' attitudes toward cooperation and competition, and their capacity and willingness to guide within the organization a sense of shared purpose, mutuality, and collegiality. It is through the leaders' conversations with their team members that this happens. Where in your network do you see this type of energy and conversation occurring?

With regard to boundary spanning, working cooperatively across multiple teams is important for the exchange of knowledge and for understanding what others know. A hot spot arises when new ideas from people in different groups and communities are brought together and knowledge sharing begins. Working across distances with people who are different from us and with people who may be strangers can lead to the most significant innovations and creative breakthroughs.

When people trust each other, feel a sense of goodwill toward one another, and are prepared and able to work across boundaries, conversations about new possibilities have the potential to produce amazing breakthrough results. Discovering an igniting purpose connects us to a desired possibility for the future.

The extent to which members within a hot spot are capable of working together in a productive manner determines the productive capacity in the hot spot formula. This is the individual group member's ability to people read and play to people's strengths across teams. What do you notice standing back from your network as you look at your willingness to work across groups, organizations, and with people you do not know well? Are you intentionally building new connections to networks that will expand your thinking? Are you exploring conversations for new possibilities?

Examine the current level of energy within your company and determine where there is potential for hot spots to emerge and where the big freeze has taken over in the clusters of community that are now showing up in your networking map.

## In Action: Karen Schannen

Karen Schannen is the vice president of Global Marketplace Insights at American Express. Building relationships with a network of people with whom she collaborates to achieve results is a large part of her day-to-day work. Her thoughts on collaboration echo several themes we've discussed.

> When I think about collaborating I think in concentric circles. The first circle is me with myself. I've got to be clear on my own goals and

where I am going. The next circle is me with my team. I need to ensure we are on the same page, focused on the same goals. Then around that circle is my team with our internal customers. We have to ensure we have the same expectations of what we are delivering. Around that is our team within our department, then the organization, and then the whole division. These concentric circles expand the importance of being able to communicate a clear set of goals and brand at each level.

When we are collaborating well we interact in ways that make us all better. I intentionally hire people who will ask me questions, challenge my thinking, make me smarter and better than I am on my own. We listen to each other, and we take actions that will build trust.

Cross department collaboration is harder that collaborating with my own team, because I am not in direct control of the goals, the time line, or the team. I intentionally think about what type of conversations I need to have to keep these relationships moving forward.

If I am not collaborating with my team members, it makes it very hard to collaborate effectively with the next circle, and so on. When that happens, an individual or a team is sunk. It is very challenging to recover from broken trust. Some people may have a passive-aggressive streak, and when you see that pattern over time, it is important to pay attention to it. Trust is vital in collaborating effectively at every level. If I do not trust an individual, team, organization, or division then I do not want to do business with them. One of the ways people deal with this is to say, "I'm too busy to work on that." When that happens, the network begins to break down.

In the past I worked with a peer who burned a bridge with his peers. He broke trust by only managing up, only looking out for himself, and being overfocused on his image. He was far too concerned with his reputation with the most senior management, and he ignored building relationships with his peers and team. Over time he proved to his peers he would stab them in the back, so people stopped working closely with him—he lost the respect he needed to get work done. That is why he did not grow in his career the way he wanted to. What he did not realize is that his reputation was that he did not have the support of his peers and his team members. That was what did him in. So the lesson I learned from living through that experience was to put more emphasis on building strong connections with your own team members and peers than on managing how you are viewed by managers above you in your network. They will hear from your team and your peers what is really happening.

## Whom Do You Want to Know?

After using your map to reflect on whom you want to know, is there anyone you want to invite to share an activity with? Perhaps you might attend an association meeting together or do something social, such as playing golf or tennis? Or maybe you are more drawn to going out for dinner, relaxing at a spa, or hosting a barbecue at your home? When you do these types of activities together, new conversations for connection, new possibilities, and new commitments bubble up.

How could you build new connections—reach out to potential collaborators who will want to strategically help you with what is on your "That's for Me!" list?

Are there activities or groups you could engage with that would enable you to live your values, reward your workplace motivators, and build new relationships?

Whom you want to listen to is often a reflection of what you are passionate about. How does this affect the relationships you have built so far? Where does it lead you for future relationships?

## Create Your Own Mastermind Team

Have you ever heard of Napoleon Hill and the classic book he wrote, *How to Think and Grow Rich*? He says the key to outstanding success is to establish a mastermind alliance. Hill defines a mastermind alliance as one that "consists of two or more people working actively together in perfect harmony toward a common definite objective." Through a mastermind

alliance, you can use the full strength of the experience, training, and knowledge of others just as if they were your own. No
individual has ever achieved huge success without the help and
cooperation of others. A group of brains coordinated in a spirit
of harmony will provide more thought energy than a single
brain, just as a group of electric batteries will provide more
energy than a single battery.

Creating a mastermind team or board of advisors is how you
may borrow and capitalize on the education and experience of
other people to help you carry out your own plans. The value
of gathering together those of a like mind who are focused on
the same goal is that a mastermind team will enable you to
accomplish in one year more than many people accomplish in a
lifetime.

Decide where you wish to be and what you wish to be doing
for the next three years. Decide how much money you want
to earn and what you are going to do to earn it. Form a
mastermind team with at least one person from your family
and at least one person who represents the type of people to
whom you want to sell your services. Offer friendly cooperation on the path of your success as you bring others along
with you.

> *Success is the knowledge with which to get whatever*
> *you want from life without violating the rights of*
> *others and by helping others to acquire it.*
> —Napoleon Hill

Henry Ford had a simple education. He had many people
working for him who had far more education than he did, more
charisma too. But he had one simple quality that they did not
possess: he was focused on how what he wanted to create would
benefit others. Henry Ford focused only on what he wanted to
create; he did not discuss, think about, or put energy into
other ideas.

*Your only real limitation is the one*
*you set up in your own mind.*
—Napoleon Hill

## Building Relationships Application Exercise

Using what you have learned early in this chapter, create your own collaboration and networking map.

Whom do you want to know?

How could you approach relationship building in new ways, based on what you learned here?

Whom do you want on your mastermind team?

What could you do to engage these people?

Use the "Book Discussion Guide" in the Appendix. Invite a group of people to discuss this book. By doing so you will be initating taking relationships to a deeper level and sharing learning.

# CHAPTER 11

# Having the Necessary Conversations and Getting the Collaboration You Want to Make Positive Changes: Tying It All Together

Think of this as the final Application Exercise as we cement the foundation and the building blocks together and provide you with a framework for inspiring collaboration and getting results. It is the person who wants change who needs to step up and adapt, who will apply what is learned here and use it to create something even better than what exists now.

Relationship building is vital to the success you want to create for yourself and others. To bring your goals and your "That's for Me!" list alive, you will want to collaborate in new ways with new people. If you want to be a leader in your organization, imagine the layers of conversations with peers and bosses that must occur before you have the credibility to be promoted to the next leadership role. Building a following requires layers of conversations in which trust develops. Once you are promoted to a leadership role then there will be another group of people you will want to build new relationships with. Each time you move into a new role or to a new level you'll want to review relationship building, your networking map, and the conversations you need to have in order to build credibility and a track record. What would your professional life look like if your "That's for Me!" list had 100 accomplishments checked off and you were on to the next round of 100 experiences you wanted to accomplish?

As you apply what you have learned here, envision the picture of your future that you would like to live. Imagine what your boss and your peers will be saying about you in a few years. How will you gain their endorsement to support you and your goals? I've guided you to recognize the conversations that take you there. What are the conversations for exploring new possibilities and conversations for structure that you need to have with yourself today, and then with others to bring this vision alive for you?

What does it look like when a team does an amazing job of collaborating, when a group of people comes together focused on a common goal that is inspiring to all of them? What happens when an individual is known for creating high-performing teams? Let me provide you with two real-life examples that answer these questions and show the highest level of endorsement.

First, I would like to introduce you to George Bickerstaff. George and I worked together when he was in an individual contributor role in a finance department of the Dun & Bradstreet Corporation. In the years since then, I've watched him collaborate with people to develop high-performing teams in many roles. George founded companies in the healthcare, financial services, social media, and information technology industries. Along the way George held senior executive roles at various Fortune 500 companies, including chief financial officer of Novartis Pharma AG ($135 billion market cap). George is well-respected for his work in philanthropic organizations, including The Global Alliance for Vaccines and Immunization

(GAVI—5 million prevented deaths since 2000). Today George plays many professional roles, including being a board member of The International Centre for Missing and Exploited Children, and the CEO of Global Innovation and the Global Leaders (the largest leadership network in the world). He is also a regular speaker and lecturer on finance, healthcare, innovation, leadership, and philanthropy. Organizations like ABC News, the Harvard Business School, Lehigh University, and UCLA invite him to share his wisdom as a guest speaker. All of this has brought him to a point where he is a recognized thought leader on business and philanthropy. Why?

I'm sharing all this detail about George's career path to highlight for you what is possible when you apply the ideas in this book. Early in his career, George made a decision to learn how to be a collaborative leader. He realized that command and control leadership does not work. George learned to people read, to adapt his communication style to the needs of the meeting or conversation at the moment, and to engage people based on their goals and aspirations. George listens, understands group dynamics, tells stories that engage others meaningfully, knows how to communicate through conflict, and how to build meaningful long-term relationships. Now, through the Global Leaders project, George helps others build networks around doing meaningful projects together. Check out what George Bickerstaff is doing in LinkedIn. Join one of his communities focused on your industry and role, and you will see a brilliant application of the key learning points from this book. What would it look like for you to build the breadth and depth to your career that George has?

Now, I'll provide another example. David L. Cohen, chairman of the University of Pennsylvania Board of Trustees, wrote this letter about Amy Gutmann and shared it publicly with the Penn Alumni community. It is an example of what can and does happen when a person establishes a positive emotional wake, creates ongoing meaningful conversations, and builds a high-performing team. A group of people creates a new vision and achieves breakthrough results through collaborating, and the leader and the team are acknowledged for the victory by being given more opportunity, money, access, and endorsements.

A Message to the Penn Community
from David L. Cohen, Chairman, Penn Board of Trustees

I am very pleased to share with you the wonderful news that President Gutmann has agreed to accept a five-year extension to her contract. This will ensure that she will continue to lead our University to at least June 30, 2019.

This is the very positive result of conversations that began several months ago and will be ratified at the meeting of the Penn Trustee Board on June 15.

Like so many who are part of the Penn community, I firmly believe that Dr. Gutmann is the best university president in the country. A summary glance at where Penn has come under her leadership is really quite amazing:

As Penn's President, Dr. Gutmann has championed greater interdisciplinary teaching and scholarship, enhancing Penn's stellar faculty by attracting world-renowned scholars, adding over 100 new named professorships, including 14 Penn Integrates Knowledge professors jointly appointed between two schools, and launching a new Action Plan for Faculty Diversity and Excellence. Penn's students are the most academically accomplished and diverse in its history. Dr. Gutmann inaugurated Penn's no-loan undergraduate financial aid program, which has greatly expanded access to a Penn education and become a model for other universities. She has led one of the most successful fundraising campaigns in higher education history, with Making History: The Campaign for Penn attaining its $3.5 billion goal 16 months ahead of schedule and securing the largest single gift in Penn history—$225 million from philanthropists Ray and Ruth Perelman. Alumni engagement has soared with participation at record high levels. Under her leadership, Penn Medicine has reached new heights in clinical care excellence and is more closely aligned with the University than at any point in its history. As one of the nation's research powerhouses, Penn's sponsored research funding has grown 23 percent to nearly $940 million annually. Through the Penn Connects master plan, Dr. Gutmann has overseen a strategic and dynamic renewal of Penn's campus, adding 47 acres—including the spectacular Penn Park and the purchase of the former DuPont Marshall Lab property—and completing nearly four million square feet of capital projects. She has played a crucial role in strengthening Penn's connections to its community, nation, and the world.

By any definition, Amy Gutmann has done a superb job.

President Gutmann is already focused on new strategic priorities for the coming years, and how we can best position Penn in a rapidly changing higher education environment. Despite the great success of the past eight years, she has made it very clear that the status quo will not suffice. I think we can all look forward to exciting new initiatives, all driven by her passionate commitment to make a Penn education the best in the world.

Being able to keep President Gutmann at the helm for another seven years is a huge win for our University. Speaking for the Trustees, I can say without reservation that we are confident that Amy has the vision and the tireless energy to sustain Penn's extraordinary momentum. I don't think there is any question that Amy Gutmann is the right person to lead us into what I know will be a very bright future.

## Final Application Exercise

What would it look like for you to build the breadth and depth to your career that George has? In what ways do you want to serve others? Answer these questions for yourself and begin to see yourself taking the next step actions you will need to take to bring this vision alive.

Imagine an amazing letter written about you or your team a year or two from now. What would you want it to say about you as a collaborator and the results you achieved with your team?

Using what you have learned from reading this book, take the time to answer that question for yourself.

What would the letter say?

How would you feel?

What would have happened just before you received the letter? What would have happened before that? Using what you
have learned from reading this book, keep asking yourself that
question until you arrive back to today. This is your unique plan
that enables you to achieve your own breakthrough by creating
new conversations and collaborating in new ways.

Congratulations on the commitment you have made to your
own professional development! By reading this book and applying what you have learned here, you are going to create a new
path for yourself and others that will enable you to be a stronger
contributor to every team you are part of going forward.

# The 12 Conversations and How to Use Them to Collaborate

Here is a brief look at each of the conversation types.

## Conversation for Connection

Connecting with others happens when we slow down enough to be in the present and really listen to one another. Rapport building requires listening now. Can you be here now? Powerful listening causes trust to grow.

## Conversation for Creating New Possibilities

Knowing what we want to create and letting ourselves dream are the first two steps in conversations for creating new possibilities. Conversations can also be the triggers to professional development. Sometimes the questions a manager or colleague asks help us to understand a situation better. We begin to see what is possible.

## Conversation for Structure

When we know what we want to create, the next step is to devise a plan. The steps in our plan might emerge one or several at a time. Nevertheless, we build our plans with the steps as we become aware of them. Maintaining forward movement is vital for long-term success.

## Conversation for Commitment

Once a plan and supporting structure are in place and we've identified action steps, we can step back and ask, "Who will execute each step?" We identify potential candidates and then seek their commitment to produce the result that corresponds with each identified task. The commitments we make to ourselves about who we want to be are the most fundamental commitments we will make.

## Conversation for Action

Once you know what you want to create, that naturally leads to a conversation about action. What do you want to *do*? What actions will make your professional dreams and goals come alive? We've all seen people get stuck in a project because they do not know what to do next. Why the quandary? They're not asking themselves the right questions.

## Conversation for Accountability

After a conversation for commitment has occurred and the expectations are clear, being accountable for engaging in what you want to do is a sign of respect. Sometimes people need to be guided into creating better outcomes.

## Conversation for Conflict Resolution

Many people do not allow themselves to recognize conflicts in their work relationships, because they simply do not know how to identify and resolve them. They sweep them under the carpet or wear blinders out of fear. Some people experience fear when the smell of conflict wafts through a conversation that doesn't offer the requisite safety. Others may overuse this conversation type and not be aware they are doing so.

## Conversation for Breakdown

Anger indicates that something or someone has crossed one of our boundaries and is a signal that we need to address the issue. Asking for what we want might clear up the breakdown. Whenever something is not working or we find ourselves oscillating, that is a breakdown. Acknowledging the breakdown is vital so that we can move forward.

## Conversation for Withdrawal and Disengagement

It is unrealistic to think that all work relationships will be enjoyable or friendly forever, and not all relationships end on a healthy, happy note. Sometimes we realize it is time to end a relationship, but the other person does not. Often it is best to end a tenuous connection, so that we can invest our time in relationships that are professionally meaningful and enjoyable.

## Conversation for Change

Your ability to change the direction of an individual, a team, or an organization occurs through conversations for change. When you need to make change happen, are you competent at guiding the necessary conversations? You can change the conversation in the office, at association meetings, at board meetings, and with peers who seem to have gone off track.

## Conversation for Appreciation

Being able to create a meaningful conversation that acknowledges and triggers feelings of appreciation is vital to building momentum in professional relationships. Think of the last time you felt really appreciated at work. What caused you to feel this way? Undoubtedly someone showed appreciation to you using language that works best for you. Affirming others is an important kind of conversation to build relationships and momentum.

## Conversation for Moving On

Chances are you have met hundreds or thousands of people in your lifetime, but you maintain close professional relationships with only a few. You have conversations for moving on when moving from a community or transferring or retiring from a company. One day you might reconnect, but for now you have closure, with no expectation of communicating again soon.

Following is a description of how to use each type of conversation when collaborating.

## Conversation for Connection

A conversation for connection is the first step in building a relationship that leads to working together to accomplish meaningful results. It enables people to understand one another's preferred communication styles. While it may initially sound like small talk, this conversation is, in fact, very important in helping us get to know each other. We can observe how others pace themselves, gesture, ask questions, listen, enunciate, and maintain eye contact. This gives us clues to their preferred communication styles. We can listen for the types of things other people want to talk about, which gives us clues to their values and motivators. It also helps us to notice when changes occur in any of these areas later, as the conversation goes deeper. Use this type of conversation when you find yourself in these situations:

Meeting new peers, employees, bosses, leaders, colleagues, or team members

Working with a new customer or a new project team

Attempting to build a solid foundation of trust, rapport, and safety

Attending a conference or company meeting

Here are some ways to get your conversation for connection started:

"How did you come to work at this organization?"

"Bob Jones suggested we connect with each other, and I wanted to reach out to you to see if we might be able to have a cup of coffee together sometime, since he thought we'd enjoy meeting each other."

"How did you meet Bob?"

"I understand you have extensive experience in . . . , and I'd love to hear about it."

"What are you passionate about?"

"I read your LinkedIn profile and noticed that we both know Sara Smith. How did you meet her?"

"Where is your accent from?"

"What are some of the current trends you are seeing in your work? How are you dealing with those trends?"

"I noticed in the newspaper this morning. . . . How will that affect you?"

"What did you enjoy studying in school, and have you been using that in your work?"

"What are some of your favorite collaboration experiences?"

"What caused you to come to this team/meeting/conference/company?"

"What projects are you currently working on?"

"How did you get into your line of work?"

"What has been your experience with LinkedIn?"

"What's new with you since we saw each other last?"

"How is your project going?"

"What's on your mind?"

"You seem excited. What's happening?"

"I am doing research about how new managers approach challenges in their work, and I know you have extensive expertise in working with project managers. Would you be willing to talk with me about this to share your experience?"

Other ways to create meaningful conversations include:

Sharing your own good news

Sharing something you learned that is interesting or useful

Telling a story that amused you

Mentioning a new product you recently tried and sharing what happened

Talking about a trend you have observed and asking if the other person has noticed it too

## Conversations for Creating New Possibilities

Product innovations, new organization structures, and new positions began with conversations for creating new possibilities. Knowing what we want to create and letting ourselves dream is the first step in having conversations for creating new possibilities. People who have made meaningful contributions have allowed themselves to think in new ways about what could be, and they have had conversations with others to engage in seeing new visions. Use this type of conversation when engaged in the following:

Trying to solve a problem that needs a new solution that is not clear to you

Brainstorming new ideas

Proposing a new idea or solution for a problem

Uncovering ideas from peers and team members

Here are some ways to get your conversation for creating new possibilities started:

"Imagine that you just won $3 million. What would you do with it?" (Let yourself play with this question as if it just happened.)

"Let's see if we can come up with 50 ideas in the next 10 minutes. No idea is too trivial or out of bounds. We are looking for volume now, and we'll come back and edit them later."

"What would you like to create?"

"If you could envision the best possible outcome, what would that look like?"

"I have an idea I'd like you to consider, and I'd be open to hearing your ideas too."

"What are the options? Can we come up with three or more options that we had not considered before?"

"If we waved a magic wand and the problem was solved, how would we know? What would be different?"

"What ideas or suggestions do you have about how we could approach this?"

"Tell me about your goals and objectives. Where do you see things going?"

"If you could be the best at one thing, what would that one thing be?"

"If you knew you would not fail, what would you do?"

"I'd like to increase the number of people who are submitting their ideas, so we have maximum user-generated content. What else could we do to invite people to submit their suggestions and ideas?"

"I appreciate your creativity. Tell me about your thoughts on how to improve or change the situation. You are welcome to be as creative as possible in exploring options."

"What do you think it will take to get there? Are there possibilities we have not yet explored?"

"Perhaps if we considered this in a new way, we could put our puzzle pieces on the table together and see what we come up with."

"Can we discuss the possibility of . . . ?"

"If there were no limitations, what resources would you need?"

"People invented the rules. When you are creating, approach it with the thought that there are no rules, or that the rules can be changed if needed. What rules are holding us back that we could consider revising?"

"What have you learned from your past that affects this situation? How can we build on that with new ideas?"

With someone who has read this book: "I'd like to have a conversation for creating new possibilities. When would be a good time for you to do that?"

## Conversation for Structure

When we know what we want to create, the next step is to create a plan for how to get there. We build our plans with the steps involved as we see them. Sometimes we only see the next step or next two steps, not the whole sequence. That's where a conversation for structure comes in. Creating a solid structure and gaining forward movement are key to success. At times we are engaged in creating the steps in the structure, and at other times we are listening to understand what the structure will be and confirming our understanding. Both of these are examples of conversations for structure.

Use this type of conversation when engaged in the following:

Establishing expectations about what will happen next

Laying out a project plan or schedule

Discussing how you will bring your goals alive

Negotiating the details of how something will be done

Ensuring that others understand the sequence of actions or events they will be involved in

Creating a process map outlining the specific steps involved

Here are some ways to get your conversation for structure started:

"What are the priorities? Of all the possibilities, what are the three most important steps that need to occur early on?"

"What structure needs to be put in place up front?"

"Which of these steps are absolutely necessary, and why?"

"Now that we are clear on the goal, how do we see this evolving?"

"What things need to happen for success?"

"Here is how we are going to move forward. . . ."

"Who are the people that need to be involved?"

"Is there a time line for the steps? When does each step need to be completed by?"

"Do we need to create a project charter or statement of work, and how will it be done? Would it be useful to put it into a visual map?"

"How will we track and measure our progress?"

"What are the cost constraints that we need to be aware of, and how do they affect our structure?"

"What are some of the best practices we could use for our structure?"

"What does the time line for deliverables look like? How often will we . . . ?"

"I am sending out the agenda prior to the meeting, so everyone knows what is expected when we are together."

"Who will keep notes, serve as the time tracker, and facilitate key discussions?"

"Have we mapped each step to the calendar to ensure that we don't have something due on a holiday or when we are all at a conference?"

"Is there a spreadsheet or data dashboard we'd like to look at weekly or monthly to track our progress?"

"Have we identified the project stakeholders and gotten their input on the steps that need to be taken?"

"Is there a specific sequence that needs to be in place?"

"What already exists that will make what we are trying to create easier? Do we need to make any changes to the existing processes to fit in with what we are doing?"

With someone who has read this book: "I'd like to have a conversation for structure. When would be a good time for you to do that?"

## Conversation for Commitment

When we have a plan or structure in place, and we've identified the action steps, we can ask, "Who will do each step?" We identify who will be responsible for each step, and then we ask each person if he or she is willing to perform it. On other occasions we realize we want to change something that will require us to commit to new actions. Perhaps the organization in which you work has made a new commitment to going green. Team leaders ask employees in departmental meetings if they will begin to use the recycle containers and stop ordering plastic bags. "Will you commit to doing your part in our green effort by using a mug instead of a plastic cup?" the manager asks each team member individually. Without this specific conversation, it is often not clear exactly what actions are expected.

Use this conversation when engaged in the following:

Being clear on what you stand for

Asking a boss or senior manager to support a proposal or idea you want to move forward with, gaining alignment among team members toward a common goal

Asking someone to play a role on your team or board, or following up from a meeting in which next actions were identified

Knowing who is responsible for what

Being clear on what it means to keep your word

Demonstrating integrity (walking your talk)

Here are some ways to get your conversation for commitment started:

"Would you be interested in these outcomes?"

"Are you willing to . . . ?"

"Can I count on you to do . . . ?"

"The reason this is so important to us is. . . . As a result, would you agree to . . . ?"

"I need help on the XYZ project. Can I count on you to do . . . ?"

"Will you be able to show Lourdes around the department on her first day next Tuesday? Will you let me know how it went when you are finished?"

"One of the commitments we made several months ago was . . . , and we are still committed to these outcomes."

"We are looking for a commitment of 20 hours dedicated to this project in the next week. Are you able to do this?"

"The proposal calls for $5,000 for the next phase in the work we want to do. Will you agree to have that come from your department budget?"

"Brian, the board has decided it would like you to lead the marketing effort. Here is an outline of the specific accountabilities expected of this role."

"When we launch a new initiative but fail to follow through, we create a cultural norm that commitment is not important. What can we do now to demonstrate we arc committed to this initiative over the next six months? How can we prompt ourselves to talk about it 6, 9, and 12 months from now to demonstrate this is not another flavor-of-the-day effort?"

## Conversation for Action

Once you have explored your options and know what you want to create and how to do it, we flow into this conversation about action. What do you need to do to bring your dreams and goals alive? After you have done that, then what will you do next? Asking these questions is a way of processing ourselves or others through our own thinking.

Use this conversation in these situations:

You have agreed to a goal and are ready to move forward.

You are ready to get things done.

You see the next step that needs to be completed.

You need to identify the next actions that need to be done to move forward.

Here are some ways to get your conversation for action started:

"What is the next action needed to move this forward?"

"What will you do next?"

"Then what? Then what?"

"What is the priority now?"

"What is the next step?"

"Imagine that failure is taken out of the picture. In other words, if you will not fail, what would you do next?"

"I've heard that, when you want to break a huge overwhelming goal down, it is useful to remember that you eat an elephant only one bite at a time. What is one step we could take that would move us forward?"

"Is there a map we could draw that would show us the sequence of action steps we want to take?"

"Let's create a checklist so we can all see the action steps in front of us and check them off individually as they are completed."

With someone who has read this book: "I'd like to have a conversation for action. When would be a good time for you to do that?"

## Conversation for Accountability

After a conversation for commitment has occurred and the expectations are clear, being accountable for what you want to do is a sign of personal respect. If other people are involved, such as when you are part of a team, being accountable is also a sign of respect toward others. Accountability brings authority and responsibility into alignment.

Use this conversation when engaged in the following:

Coaching an employee, peer, or colleague to stay focused on the previously defined goals

Debriefing a team on what has been accomplished

Reviewing your own goals and commitments

Spinning around with a goal that has not yet moved forward

Holding yourself accountable for what you agreed to do

Holding others accountable for what they agreed to do

Talking about the impact when others do not live up to their promises

## A Six-Step Plan for Confronting Others

Are you speaking up in a solution-focused manner when you notice something that could be improved? Does your organization encourage you to have Conversations for Accountability? Have you distinguished what causes some conversations for accountability to be more productive than others? Elizabeth Jeffries, an executive coach who focuses on executive mastery and works with me at The Professional Development Group, shares a six-step plan she uses to prepare for a conversation for accountability. The plan is a multipurpose approach to dealing with other people's negative, ineffective, or unacceptable behavior. Sometimes you have to have a confrontation in order to see changes in behavior.

1. Approach the person with an attitude of solving a problem, rather than one of putting the person down. Do it at a time when you are in control of your emotions. This is the mental preparation step.
2. Describe the person's behavior objectively. "I have noticed . . ."
3. Express your feelings and thoughts about the person's behavior. "I feel angry and frustrated."
4. Suggest a specific change in behavior. "I'd prefer . . ." "May I suggest . . ."
5. Explain the benefits that will result from the new behavior. "I'll be more open to your ideas . . ." "If you will do that, we'll both be more effective in our work."
6. Ask for commitment to the new behavior. "What would it take for you to . . . ?" "Will you agree to this?" "Can I count on you?" If yes, ask, "How would I know?" (the accountability statement)

Here are some ways to get your conversation for accountability started:

"I'd like to review the goals and where we are with them."

"What will it look like if this goal is completed well?"

"How will we hold each other accountable for these goals?"

"What will be done by the end of the day today?"

"When will you have this ready for the client?"

"Do you have time next Tuesday to discuss your goals and what progress has been made against them?"

"I'm concerned we may have had a misunderstanding, and I'd like to get on the same page with you about what the intention really is."

"How can I be helpful to you in reaching the agreed-upon deliverable?"

"How will I know when it has been completed?"

"Let's establish milestone dates to review the objectives and what we've accomplished thus far."

"What other tools or resources are needed to ensure your success?"

"Will you e-mail me when you have finished this, so I can move forward with the next part?"

"Shall we talk every day around 5:00 p.m. to discuss what was completed that day?"

"Will you let me know if there is something holding you back from progressing to the next step as soon as you are aware of it, so we can think out the options together?"

"How often would you like me to check in with you to ensure you are on track?"

"What gets measured gets done. Are we measuring what we want as outcomes?"

"Is there another way we could approach accountability on this project that we have not yet discussed?"

With someone who has read this book: "I'd like to have a conversation for accountability. When would be a good time for you to do that?"

## Conversation for Conflict Resolution

If we do not admit there is an issue, we cannot resolve a conflict. If we take on the mindset of someone who is exploring to learn and seek out new ways of viewing things, then we will be open to exploring possibilities for resolving conflicts. Being in a conflict does not necessarily mean that a fight is occurring or that it is obvious to others. Many useful products and services were born out of recognizing differences in needs, discussing unmet needs, and working through the underlying conflict to resolve issues. If we are not stepping up to deal with unresolved conflict on the teams we lead, the team members will begin to lose respect for our management capabilities. Respect from others often comes once they have seen that we are willing to deal with conflict in productive ways. When we are too passive in avoiding an issue, it would be helpful to look under that behavior at what the feeling is.

Often we will discover that fear is holding us back from speaking up about what we need to discuss. Forcing ourselves out of a comfort zone may help us to notice conflicts and speak up about them in ways that lead to a solution. The most successful conflict facilitators understand the other side's concerns and needs as much as they understand their own. They ask questions and carefully listen, so that the other side sees the willingness for mutual exploration and problem-solving dialogue. It is debilitating to be filled with anger and fear from unacknowledged conflict or conflict that is habitually ignored. Although we cannot make others change when they are not willing to, we can invite them to explore the effects of new possibilities, even if they are resistant to it.

When people are trying to end a conflict or an injustice they feel they are suffering, they need to understand the other party too. If they do not do this, they are focusing on themselves and not on the real issue. This is what creates victim-like circular thinking. If you feel you are stuck in a no-win situation, it is worth looking at your own circular thinking, which is creating the victim pattern. Seek out role models who have worked through conflict successfully. Be open to their observation and feedback about your thinking and what you could do to create a solution.

Use this type of conversation in these situations:

Someone is ignoring an issue that is important to you.

You notice yourself ignoring an issue that is important to someone who is a stakeholder in your work.

You need to express differences and disappointments with someone.

There is chronic tension in a relationship.

You need to find a path to agreement.

You want to agree to disagree, without hiding your disagreement and then later acting in a passive-aggressive or hostile way.

You feel anger, bitterness, or resentment.

You notice someone else is angry, bitter, or resentful.

Here are some ways to get your conversation for conflict resolution started:

"I'd like to hear more about your perspective and feelings. Would you be willing to share more, so I can better understand your perspective?"

"We may see things differently here, and I'd like to explore what we agree on as well as where we are viewing things differently. Would you be willing to start with where we have agreement?"

"Sometimes it is useful to agree to disagree and move on. Are we in one of those situations? Are we both able to move on and let this go, so it is not preventing us from doing the next action?"

"I'd like to invite you to have coffee off-site sometime next week. I am struggling with something, and I would really appreciate the opportunity to discuss it with you to get your input."

"I have a commitment to focus on the desired behavior and outcomes we'd like to create, rather than focusing on what we don't want. Will you join me in this?"

"What would you need for us to work through this issue?"

"What are the values underlying your needs in this situation?"

"Is there something we are tiptoeing around that we would both benefit by discussing?"

"I'm conflicted about an issue, and I'd like to talk it out with someone who is unbiased, who will ask me questions to get me thinking in new ways. Will you be that person?"

## Conversation for Breakdown

Sometimes one type of conversation leads us into another type naturally. If a conversation for conflict resolution does not produce results and it seems as though we've tried just about everything, then we need to acknowledge the severity of the conflict and move on, rather than wallowing in the conflict. A breakdown occurs when things are not working and we are in an oscillating pattern. Acknowledging the breakdown is the first step. Just admitting to yourself that you are in a breakdown around an issue can cause you to let go of the resistance and trigger a move into a new conversation.

Use this type of conversation in these situations:

You feel jammed up, stuck, afraid, and unable to think clearly.

You notice yourself or someone else caught in circular thinking that is not creating what is needed next.

A person or team is not meeting his or her, or its goals.

You are admitting you do not know what to do next.

You are ready to move through the stuck places.

Here are some ways to get your conversation for breakdown started:

"Is it possible for me to put this all in the drawer for a few hours and step away from it, perhaps go for a long walk, visit with a friend, or take a hot bath, and then revisit this situation determined to get unstuck, with clarity about what I want to do next?"

"We have a commitment to do . . . , but we have not been able to move in that direction. What is it that is keeping us from moving forward?"

"It seems to me like we are stuck. Do you see it that way too?"

"If someone else were looking at this situation, would that person say we are oscillating instead of moving forward?"

"Let's take 24 hours to think this through and determine whether we should move forward with this decision."

"It seems to me that we are in need of a conversation to acknowledge our breakdown. Do you agree?"

## Conversation for Withdrawal and Disengagement

You may be wondering why in a book about collaborating and getting results I included a conversation focused on withdrawal and disengagement. It's because sometimes our best efforts to collaborate do not work, and we realize our values and motivators are too far off for us to be able to be effective together. How can we disengage with as much self-esteem and respect for the other parties as possible? Not all relationships need to go forward. Sometimes, when things just are not working out, we have to take a step back and disengage from a colleague, a team, or business partner. When we realize this is the case, how can we end on a healthy, respectful note?

Use this type of conversation in these situations:

You realize a relationship is a no-win situation for anyone.

There is nothing you can do to help or support a team member in moving forward with his or her current goals.

You are stuck in a pattern of anger, sadness, or fear with a boss, team, or group.

It is time to move on.

You recognize when a conversation or relationship does not need to move forward.

It's time to admit that a relationship is toxic.

You realize you need to let go when the other party is not letting go (he or she is clinging on out of fear or need, and it is not healthy for either of you).

Here are some ways to get your conversation for withdrawal and disengagement started:

"Thank you for the opportunity to work with you. I've learned so much while I was here. It is now time for me to move on and continue my learning, though."

"This is no longer working for me, and I've decided to make a change for myself. It is not a move against you; it is a step ahead for me."

"I have another opportunity that I want to explore at this time."

"This role no longer fits with my vision and values for my career. As a result, I need to make a change for myself."

"I've decided I need to make some changes for myself. My changes have an impact on you and our working relationship, so I wanted to make you aware of what I am doing."

"I am choosing to narrow my client list to my top three clients. Unfortunately that means I'd like to transition our work over to another person."

## Conversation for Change

If what you are doing is getting the results you want, keep doing it. If not, it is time to step up and make a change. Change is an individual choice. When we choose to change our behavior and beliefs, or the behavior of other people, then our conversations will have to change too. We have to bring others along to understand how we went from one way of thinking or operating to another way, and why they may want to as well. The way to do this is with a conversation for change. This is what Gandhi meant when he said, "Let us be the change we want to see in the world." If we do not have a conversation that helps others to understand the change in our thinking, we create a gap between ourselves and other people. We have to show others that we have changed so they can join in too.

Use this type of conversation in these situations:

A new leader joins the organization or team.

A significant change is needed or has just occurred.

A team member's performance is not meeting expectations.

Your boundaries need to be changed or reinforced.

You want open dialogue about current reality and the desired state.

You are undertaking a new mission.

Here are some ways to get your conversation for change started:

"I notice what seems like shifting sands, and I want to check it out with you to see if you are experiencing these changes as well."

"I have a dream that we could . . ."

"A vision that really inspires me is . . ."

"What would need to exist for us to embrace the new vision?"

"Google and Apple created positive change, and I think we can too, if we . . ."

"What would it look like if we were the best in . . . ?"

"Is there anything I need to forgive, so I can be present in the moment now?"

"Current reality is calling us to make some changes. Let's talk about what our experience of current reality is and how we can respond to it."

"What have you noticed changing?"

"Are there trends that are occurring around us that we have not yet discussed?"

"If we got in front of the changes that we think are coming, what would it look like?"

"How could we be proactive, instead of reactive, in this situation?"

"What else do we think needs to change and why?"

"What would we like the 'new normal' to be?"

"How has another industry or business dealt with a current reality like the one we are experiencing now? What was the impact of the way they handled it?"

"There is no such thing as 'We are all stable and will continue to be for years to come.' In light of this fact, I'd like to share some observations I have about trends that I think will lead to changes we need to be prepared for."

"Can we learn from someone else's experience?"

"Do you ever find yourself saying something like 'Once we get through this crazy period of change, then everything will return to normal'? I've realized that this belief is a problem, because we will be faced with ongoing change. In fact, a trend I see that will bring about another round of change is . . .'"

"Our frenzied pace of change is the new 'normal.' Let's identify ways we can do a better job of helping others on our team to understand why this is the truth so we can all become energized by the exciting possibilities offered by the changes."

## Conversation for Appreciation

A little appreciation goes a long way. (With that in mind, allow me to take a moment to thank you for sticking with me through these chapters.) Conversations for appreciation are uplifting deposits into the emotional bank account between people. You have likely created many of these in the past. They specifically acknowledge the contributions others have made. I hope you have not waited until now to create a conversation for appreciation. These conversations can be used anytime you sincerely want to express gratitude. They can be built into some of the previous conversations that may have several meetings to get to resolution.

Use this type of conversation in these situations:

You are developing new skills in yourself or others.

You are grateful for the progress that has been made.

You want to say thank you in a meaningful way.

You want to customize your appreciation to the style of the person you are thanking.

You want a stronger relationship that generates endorsement from another person or a group.

You are endorsing others.

Here are some ways to get your conversation for appreciation started:

"Thank you for . . ."

"The reason I really appreciate what you did is . . ."

"I wanted to point out several things I've noticed that you have done very well recently . . ."

"Philip told me you really excel at . . ."

"Kiki, while Hiromi is standing here with us, I wanted to share with you some of the things that he has done recently to help our department. He has been a star because he . . ."

"Congratulations on the successful completion of the XYZ project. Thank you for putting in so much time to ensure that all the details were handled."

"What a great event you pulled off. I really enjoyed the . . ."

"I can see you are going to be just what we need in this organization. I'm glad you are joining us."

"That was the best meeting we've had. Thank you for doing such a good job facilitating our team meeting. You got everyone participating by asking such great questions, Lisa."

"Thank you for doing your best on this webinar. I really liked the way you . . ."

"I am writing you this thank-you note because I wanted you to know how much it meant to us that you . . ."

"Because appreciation is so personal and I want to do something nice to acknowledge you, I'd like to know what your favorite restaurant is, so I can treat you to lunch to thank you for . . ."

## Conversation for Moving On

Moving to a new office space, retiring from a company, and taking a position with another company are examples of times when we have conversations for moving on. Good-bye parties or lunches are a nice way to acknowledge when someone is withdrawing in a healthy way. We let go and move on, perhaps remembering one another with a friendly holiday or birthday card each year.

Use this type of conversation in these situations:

Someone is moving, retiring, or leaving the team, and you want to share how he or she contributed.

A project is ending.

You do not want to burn a bridge, and you would like the relationship to continue, even though you will not be seeing each other regularly any more.

You want to summarize what was done or acknowledge what was accomplished.

It's time to let go of the current structure for how you connect.

You want to create healthy endings.

You are moving on.

Here are some ways to get your conversation for moving on started:

"I wanted to take a few minutes to acknowledge our work together on the XYZ team as we prepare to move on."

"You made an impact on this project by doing . . ."

"Thank you for all the effort you put into . . . I wish you all success in future projects."

"You are my new role model for integrity, and I wanted to share with you an example of something you did that causes me to say this . . . May I connect with you again, when I am on another project and need you as a role model?"

"The next time I need help with . . . , I'd like to call you to see if you are available."

"Perhaps you'd like me to introduce you to Donna, who is also passionate about . . . The two of you would enjoy knowing each other, now that you have more free time on your hands."

## Book Discussion Guide

Business discussion groups provide a forum for teams to share learning together. I highly recommend joining a Business Banter group or starting one yourself. I lead two of these groups. One is for an executive team that wants to get on the same page and share experiences, The other one is at a country club to engage members in getting to know each other. Both have been very successful in providing like-minded people with the opportunity to share and learning together as a group. If you have not participated in such a group, consider using this book as your launch point. Look at your networking map and identify 6 to 12 people you would enjoy discussing this book with. Invite them to meet over coffee, lunch, or dinner. Use the following questions as a discussion guide for each chapter:

## Part 1: The Foundation for Successful Collaboration

### Chapter 1: Knowing What You Want to Create

- What was the outcome of you creating your own "That's for Me!" list?
- What do you want to create?
- What happens to people who are not clear about what they want to create?
- What insights did you have from doing the "Knowing What You Want to Create Application Exercise"?

### Chapter 2: People Reading: Preferred Communication Styles

- Which communication style do you prefer?
- Which one or ones are most challenging for you?
- Could you relate to Tamara's story?
- Have you experienced the predictable patterns that sabotage effective collaboration—if so, how do you handle these now?
- What did you gain from doing the "People Reading: Preferred Communication Styles Application Exercise"?

### Chapter 3: People Reading: Motivators

- What are your motivators?
- What are your organization's motivators?
- Do you have alignment?

### Chapter 4: People Reading: Emotional Intelligence

- What was your reaction to the EQ competencies—self-awareness, self-regulation, motivation, empathy, and social skills?
- Share your own experiences from doing the "People Reading: Emotional Intelligence Application Exercise."

### Chapter 5: Tying Together People Reading

- Could you relate to Anya's story and Jacqueline and Ben's story?
- How did you implement the suggestion to practice people reading?
- What was the outcome?

### Part 2: The Building Blocks for Successful Collaborations That Get Results

### Chapter 6: Deep Listening

- What resonated with you in this chapter?
- In what ways have you noticed your beliefs affecting your listening?
- How did you relate to Stuart's story?
- How have you handled situations when a team member, peer, or boss is not listening to you?
- Have you noticed what others do to gain your attention?

## Chapter 7: Relationship and Group Dynamics That Affect Collaboration

Which of the following ideas in this chapter caused aha moments for you?

- Partnership and enmeshment
- Decision-making power and control
- Teresa's group decision-making story
- Overfunctioning and underfunctioning
- Changing patterns
- Levels of maturity
- Emergent leader roles
- Stages of team development
- Schedule chicken

## Chapter 8: Storytelling

- What have you observed about the story plots you use most?
- Could you relate to Jenny's, Collin's, or Paul's stories?

## Chapter 9: When Conflict Stops Progress: Creating More Effective Conversations, That Lead to Resolution

- What were you insights from this chapter about the causes of conflicts?
- Have you observed the common mistakes in resolving conflict?
- How have you used the ideas from this chapter? What did you learn from doing the "Conflict Resolution Application Exercise"?

## Chapter 10: Relationship Building

- What did you recognize from building your collaboration and networking map?
- Who do you want to know?
- What is your reaction to the suggestion to create your own mastermind team?

## Chapter 11: Having the Necessary Conversations and Getting the Collaboration You Want

- How do you relate to the success stories?
- What resonated with you from the "Final Application Exercise"?
- How will you keep this learning alive and in action?

Updates and additional resources can be found online at www.YourTalentAtWork.com. Contact Shawn Kent Hayashi at The Professional Development Group: e-mail info@ TheProfessionalDevelopmentGroup.com or call 888-959-1188.

# Index

# About the Author

**Shawn Kent Hayashi** is the founder and CEO of the Professional Development Group. Her clients include Fortune 500 companies, universities, and entrepreneurial organizations.